Landmarks of world literature

Jonathan Swift

GULLIVER'S TRAVELS

Landmarks of world literature

General editor: J. P. Stern

Dickens: *Bleak House* — Graham Storey
Homer: *The Iliad* — Michael Silk
Dante: *The Divine Comedy* — Robin Kirkpatrick
Balzac: *Old Goriot* — David Bellos
Mann: *Buddenbrooks* — Hugh Ridley
Homer: *The Odyssey* — Jasper Griffin
Tolstoy: *Anna Karenina* — Anthony Thorlby
Conrad: *Nostromo* — Ian Watt
Camus: *The Stranger* — Patrick McCarthy
Murasaki Shikibu: *The Tale of Genji* — Richard Bowring
Sterne: *Tristram Shandy* — Wolfgang Iser
Shakespeare: *Hamlet* — Paul A. Cantor
Stendhal: *The Red and the Black* — Stirling Haig
Pasternak: *Doctor Zhivago* — Angela Livingstone
Proust: *Swann's Way* — Sheila Stern
Pound: *The Cantos* — George Kearns
Beckett: *Waiting for Godot* — Lawrence Graver
Chaucer: *The Canterbury Tales* — Winthrop Wetherbee
Virgil: *The Aeneid* — K.W. Gransden
García Márquez: *One Hundred Years of Solitude* — Michael Wood
Cervantes: *Don Quixote* — A.J. Close
Céline: *Journey to the End of the Night* — John Sturrock
Boccaccio: *Decameron* — David Wallace
Wordsworth: *The Prelude* — Stephen Gill
Eliot: *Middlemarch* — Karen Chase
Hardy: *Tess of the d'Urbervilles* — Dale Kramer
The Bible — Stephen Prickett and Robert Barnes
Flaubert: *Madame Bovary* — Stephen Heath
Baudelaire: *Les Fleurs du mal* — F.W. Leakey
Zola: *L'Assommoir* — David Baguley
Boswell: *The Life of Johnson* — Greg Clingham
Pushkin: *Eugene Onegin* — A.D.P. Briggs
Dostoyevsky: *The Brothers Karamazov* — W.J. Leatherbarrow
Galdós: *Fortunata and Jacinta* — Harriet S. Turner
Aeschylus: *The Oresteia* — Simon Goldhill
Byron: *Don Juan* — Anne Barton
Lawrence: *Sons and Lovers* — M.H. Black
Swift: *Gulliver's Travels* — Howard Erskine-Hill
Milton: *Paradise Lost* — David Loewenstein

JONATHAN SWIFT

Gulliver's Travels

HOWARD ERSKINE-HILL

*Reader in Literary History in the Faculty of English,
University of Cambridge, and Fellow of Pembroke
College*

CAMBRIDGE
UNIVERSITY PRESS

Published by the Press Syndicate of the University of Cambridge
The Pitt Building, Trumpington Street, Cambridge CB2 1RP
40 West 20th Street, New York NY 10011-4211, USA
10 Stamford Road, Oakleigh, Melbourne 3166, Australia

First published 1993

Printed and bound in Great Britain by
Woolnough Bookbinding Ltd, Irthlingborough, Northamptonshire

A catalogue record for this book is available from the British Library

Library of Congress cataloguing in publication data

Erskine-Hill, Howard
Jonathan Swift: Gulliver's travels / Howard Erskine-Hill.
    p.   cm. – (Landmarks of world literature)
Includes index.
ISBN 0 521 32934 5 (hardback)
1. Swift, Jonathan, 1667–1745. Gulliver's travels.
I. Title.   II. Series.
PR3724.G8E75 1993
823'.5 – dc20   92-36786 CIP

ISBN 0 521 32934 5 hardback
ISBN 0 521 33842 5 paperback

WG

To my undergraduate pupils at Cambridge

Contents

Acknowledgements   *page* viii
Textual note   ix
Chronology   x

1   Introduction   1

2   Different kingdoms, different parties   3

3   Marvels and voyages   11

4   A voyage to Lilliput   22

5   A voyage to Brobdingnag   37

6   A voyage to Laputa, Balnibarbi, Luggnag,
    Glubbdubdrib, and Japan   48

7   A voyage to the country of the Houyhnhnms   61

8   Concluding   80

9   The fictional aftermath   94

Guide to further reading   105

Acknowledgements

I gratefully acknowledge my debt to Paul Turner's edition of
Gulliver's Travels (Oxford, 1971) and to the critics and scholars
listed in the Guide to further reading. Having taught and
discussed the *Travels* in universities for over thirty years, I am
haunted by the probability of forgotten indebtedness, and put
on record here my apologies and gratitude to The Unacknow-
ledged Scholar.

I wish to acknowledge in addition conversations with my
colleague, the late Miss I. M. Westcott, who first revealed to
me something of the political complexity of More's *Utopia*, and
who suggested to me the notion of double vision in *Gulliver's
Travels*. I am grateful to Saul Rosenberg for talking to me
about Dampier, and Timothy Underhill for drawing my attention to John Flavell.

Textual note

Quotations from *Gulliver's Travels* are from Paul Turner's edition, henceforth referred to as Turner. References after quotations give first Swift's own Part and chapter numbers; then page numbers in Turner. Readers using other editions should thus find it easy to locate any quotation. Other works referred to in abbreviated form in the text are cited fully in the Guide to further reading.

Chronology

	Public events	Literary events	Events in the life of Swift
1516		Thomas More's *Utopia*	
1532–64		François Rabelais, *Gargantua and Pantagruel*	
1534	Henry VIII breaks with the Roman Catholic Church		
1535	Execution of Thomas More, Saint in the Roman Catholic Church (1935)		
1547	Accession of Edward VI. Protestantism more firmly established		
1553	Accession of Mary I. Roman Catholicism reinstated		
1558	Accession of Elizabeth I. Protestantism reinstated		
1589		Richard Hakluyt, *Principle Navigations, Voyages and Discoveries*	
1603	Accession of James VI of Scotland as James I. Episcopalian form of Protestantism confirmed in England		
1605		Francis Bacon, *Advancement of Learning*	
1609		Joseph Hall, *Mundus Alter et Idem*	

	Historical events	Literary works	Swift's life
1625	Accession of Charles I		
1626		Francis Bacon, *The New Atlantis*	
1637		René Descartes, *Discours de la Méthode*; Descartes, *Méditations Metaphysique*	
1641			
1642	Civil War		
1649	Execution of Charles I, Blessed Martyr in the Anglican Church. Accession of Charles II *de jure*		
1657		Cyrano de Bergerac, *Histoire Comique ... de la Lune*	
1660	Restoration of Charles II. Establishment of Anglican, Episcopal, Church in England, Ireland and Scotland		
1667		Milton, *Paradise Lost*; Dryden, *Annus Mirabilis*	30 November, Swift born to English parents, in Dublin
1671		Milton, *Paradise Regained* and *Samson Agonistes*	
1673			Swift attends Kilkenny Grammar School
1676		Gabriel de Foigny, *La Terre Australe Connue*	
1678		John Bunyan, *The Pilgrim's Progress*	
1680		Rochester, *Poems*	
1681		Dryden, *Absalom and Achitophel*	
1682			Matriculates at Trinity College Dublin (BA 1686)

1685	Accession of James II, a Roman Catholic	
1687		Dryden, *The Hind and the Panther*
1688	Invasion of William, Prince of Orange. Expulsion of James II. Civil War	
1689	William and Mary II come to the throne. War with France (War of the League of Augsburg)	Swift flees Ireland to visit his mother in Leicester
		Becomes Secretary to Sir William Temple, at Moor Park, Surrey
		Returns briefly to Ireland
1690	William III defeats James II at the Battle of the Boyne	
1691		Authorized version of Rochester's *Poems*
1692	Defeat and withdrawal of Jacobite forces in Ireland	MA Oxford
1693		William Congreve's *Old Bachelor* and *Double-Dealer*
1694	Death of Mary II. Triennial Act. Founding of Bank of England	
1695		Congreve, *Love for Love*
		Returns to Dublin, is ordained in the Anglican Church and secures the living of Kilroot, near Belfast
1696	Jacobite Assassination Plot against William III	
1697	Treaty of Ryswick halts the European War	Dryden publishes his verse translation of the *Works of Virgil*.

1697		William Dampier publishes *A New Voyage Round the World*	
1699			Death of Temple. Swift Chaplain to the Earl of Berkeley, Dublin
1700		Dryden publishes his *Fables Ancient and Modern*. Death of Dryden. Congreve, *The Way of the World*	Vicar of Laracor, and Prebendary of St Patrick's Cathedral, Dublin
1701	Death of James II. Accession of James III *de jure*		
1702	Death of William III. Accession of Anne. War of the Spanish Succession. Formation of a Tory Ministry		
1704			Publishes *A Tale of a Tub*, *The Battle of the Books* and *The Mechanical Operation of the Spirit*
1705	Tory Ministry collapses		
1707	Robert Harley begins to construct a mixed Administration		
1708	Jacobite invasion attempt		Swift publishes the *Bickerstaff Papers*
1709		Alexander Pope publishes his *Pastorals*. Richard Steele publishes *The Tatler*	Swift returns to Ireland
1710	Tory success in General Elections. New Tory administration under Robert Harley and Henry St John		Back in England, publishes *The Examiner* on behalf of the Tory administration
1710–14			*Journal to Stella*

1711		Pope publishes *An Essay on Criticism*. Joseph Addison publishes *The Spectator*	Publishes *An Argument against Abolishing Christianity*, and *The Conduct of the Allies* in support of the Tory Peace
1712		John Arbuthnot publishes *The History of John Bull*. Pope publishes two-canto version of *The Rape of the Lock*	
1713	Treaty of Utrecht ends War of the Spanish Succession	Pope publishes *Windsor Forest* to celebrate the Peace	Swift installed as Dean of St Patrick's Cathedral, Dublin
1714	Death of Anne. George I comes to the throne. Whig administration installed	Five-canto version of *The Rape of the Lock*. Mandeville's *Fable of the Bees*	Swift returns to Dublin
1715	Civil War in England and Scotland Harley imprisoned in the Tower. St John and Ormonde escape to France	Addison publishes *The Freeholder*. Pope publishes *The Temple of Fame*. *Iliad* translation, I–IV	
1716	Septennial Act		
1717	Gyllenborg Plot on behalf of James III	*Three Hours After Marriage*, by Gay and Arbuthnot. Pope publishes his collect *Works*	
1719	Spanish troops land in Scotland on behalf of James III	Daniel Defoe, *Robinson Crusoe*. Pope at work on his collaborative *Odyssey* translation	
1719–27			Swift composes his poems to Stella
1720	South-Sea Bubble Crisis. Robert Walpole heads new Whig administration		Swift publishes his *Proposal for Use of Irish Manufacture*

1722	Atterbury Conspiracy on behalf of James III		
1723	Atterbury exiled. St John buys his return	Pope publishes his *Odyssey* translation, I–III	
1724	Crisis concerning a new currency in Ireland		*Drapier's Letters*
1726			Swift revisits England with the MS of *Gulliver's Travels*, which is published anonymously
1727	Accession of George II. Walpole survives as premier	Pope–Swift *Miscellanies*, I and II	Swift's last visit to England
1728		Gay's *Beggar's Opera*. Pope's *Dunciad*.	
1729		Pope's *Dunciad Variorum*, with its address to Swift in Bk I. Pope's *An Essay on Man*, I–III	Swift's *A Modest Proposal*
1731			Swift writes *Verses on the Death of Dr Swift*
1733	Excise Bill crisis		
1734		Pope completes *An Essay on Man*	
1735		Pope's Epistle *To Dr Arbuthnot*	Faulkner publishes Swift's *Works*, with corrected edition of *Gulliver's Travels*
1737			
1738		Samuel Johnson's *London*	
1739	War of Jenkins' Ear		

1740		War of the Austrian Succession
1741	Pope publishes *Memoirs of Martinus Scriblerus*	
1742	Handel's *Messiah*	Fall of Walpole
	Swift falls seriously ill of orbital cellulitis and a series of minor strokes. These, with his earlier complaint of Ménière's disease, cause him to be regarded as of 'unsound mind'.	
1743	Pope publishes *The Dunciad* in four books	
1744	Death of Pope	French naval attempt on Britain on behalf of James III
1745		Civil War in Scotland and England
	Swift dies on 19 October, and is privately buried in St Patrick's Cathedral. In his will he left £11,000 to establish a hospital for the insane	

Chapter 1

Introduction

Anyone who makes a statement about Swift's *Travels Into Several Remote Nations of the World. In Four Parts. By Lemuel Gulliver* ... must soon expect to be confronted by a counter-statement perhaps equally plausible. That is the nature of Swift's book. It studies paradox and dilemma. The present monograph is nevertheless rash enough to aim at several specific goals. First, it seeks to focus upon the extraordinary narrative and imaginative achievement of the *Travels* which has too often been pushed to the margins of debate by a body of criticism largely concerned with satiric intention and final effect. That kind of criticism is, of course, provoked by the text and would have given Swift much wry satisfaction. The hermeneutic battles, especially on the significance of Part IV, are of great interest, yet they take us surprisingly far from the reading experience of the *Travels* upon which final interpretation must, in the last analysis, rest.

Secondly, I argue that the centre of Swift's art in this book is an ironic viewpoint: to be specific, the purposely unpredictable variation in relation between Gulliver and the reader, sometimes near identification, sometimes morally distanced. This sequence of significant involvement and detachment, evolved and intensified as it is, is a function of the complementary relation of Part and Part. The continuity of Gulliver as a simple and knowable character is essential to this, for change cannot be recognized as significant without a thread of continuity. The changing relation between Gulliver and reader is what makes the *Travels* so much more than merely a devastating attack on 'that Animal called man' which we might witness with shock, wonder and distaste. Swift's handling of Gulliver has a rhetorical design on the reader, lies in ambush for us, making the judgement of others quite inescapably and

1

painfully the judgement of ourselves, and making us undergo all the emotions, gratifying or mortifying, of judging and being judged. It is tempting to argue that, by virtue of its ironic viewpoint, *Gulliver's Travels* is a landmark in literature. But here the Cervantes of *Don Quixote* has come before. Rather the *Travels* is a landmark for the power with which it turns ironic viewpoint against passivities and complacencies of its readers.

Thirdly, I question the traditional and now almost automatic opinion that Part III of the *Travels* is inferior to the other Parts; and hope to demonstrate the crucial importance of Part III to the design of the whole work.

Finally, I suggest that a great part of Swift's ironic reserve in the presentation of humanity through Gulliver and his travels concerns this character's pointed lack of any but a nominal Christianity, so that the eighteenth-century reader would, to all intents and purposes, have seen Gulliver as a man without religion. This is not to claim that such religion would have been incompatible with an admiration for the Houyhnhnms. A part of this ironic reserve concerning Gulliver as, in effect, an irreligious man involves his attitude to his trustworthy and loving wife, in which connection I suggest a reason for Gulliver's Christian (that is, his given) name.

A short discussion is appended of the creative reception of *Gulliver's Travels* from 1726 to our own time.

Chapter 2

Different kingdoms, different parties

Gulliver's Travels may by general agreement be about difficulties of identity and problems of judgement. But its means to the exposure of these difficulties and problems are descriptions of how people live together in communities of different kinds, how they are governed, or how they govern themselves. Thus the political and social events of Swift's age have a claim on our attention, for the 'civil Commotions' which Principal Secretary Reldresal informs Gulliver of in the Empire of Lilliput (I. 4) may in principle stem from the civil commotions of the kingdoms into which Swift was born and have, in their turn, a bearing on the whole history of his time.

'The meaning of Swift's work will escape anybody who forgets that his English career, long and important as it was, only interrupted an Irish life' (Ehrenpreis, *Swift*, I. 8). This claim by Swift's leading biographer in the later twentieth century is clearly important, the more important since historians now propose that the civil wars of the seventeenth century arose as much from the distinctness of the three kingdoms of the British monarchy as from general economic or ideological causes (Russell, *Causes*, pp. 26–8). Swift grew to young manhood mainly in Ireland, in the aftermath of both the devastating Cromwellian civil war in that kingdom, and of the precarious restoration of the monarchy and episcopal Anglican Church in all three kingdoms in 1660. Associated with the Protestant Ascendancy in predominantly Roman Catholic Ireland, Swift saw a Roman Catholic monarch, James II and VII, begin to introduce pro-Catholic legislation, and thus provoke the defiance, in England, of the Seven Bishops of the established Church. He saw King James lose control of the political situation in the face of the expedition of the Prince of Orange, in 1688, but then found himself surrounded in his last year as

3

a junior member of Trinity College, Dublin, by an Ireland almost all under the control of James II's Deputy, the Earl of Tyrconnel. Soon James himself would land there, and a pro-Catholic parliament sit in Dublin. In Scotland too there was civil war: only in England, the country of Swift's Anglican forebears, did the throne seem to have changed hands in peace.

Swift fled papist Ireland, to visit his mother in England, and to seek a career in the larger, more stable kingdom. He was later said to have considered Joseph the most 'distinguished' character in the Old Testament (Delaney, *Observations*, p. 33) and it is interesting that Joseph like Swift survived danger at home to become great in another land, and like Swift was faithful to his earliest connections.

The Swifts were slightly linked with two powerful Irish families, those of James Butler, Duke of Ormonde and Sir William Temple, retired diplomat and man of letters. Temple now offered Swift a post in his household at Moor Park, near Farnham. Despite a series of visits back to Ireland where by 1690 Jacobitism was in retreat after a series of major battles, Swift remained with Temple for most of the 1690s, even after his ordination into the Established Church and preferment to the living of Kilroot, near Belfast, in 1695. Swift's earliest contact with the inner world of high politics is likely to have been in discussions with Temple, whose career had been a curious pattern of disappointment and success. As Charles II's ambassador to the United Provinces, Temple had observed at first hand the most successful republic of the age. He framed the Triple Alliance between the United Provinces, Britain and Sweden, only to be systematically deceived by his master's prior and covert commitment to France. A trusted adviser of William of Orange, he encouraged that prince's marriage with Princess Mary, daughter of James II when Duke of York, thus giving William his claim to the throne in 1688. Swift who always referred with respect to Temple, probably shared many of his views on these matters of state. Yet the complexity of his own reactions may be judged from the fact that of his early odes, then unpublished, one was 'to the King. On his Irish Expedition. And The Success of his Arms in general', another 'to Dr William Sancroft', the deprived Archbishop of Canterbury who, having defied James II, nevertheless refused to take the Oaths to William.

The 1690s saw Swift's composition of the brilliant anonymous volume comprising *A Tale of a Tub*, *The Battle of the Books* and *The Mechanical Operation of the Spirit*, which was published in 1704. For many Swiftians this volume contains his greatest and most original satire, though the astonishing *Tale of a Tub* has never achieved the fame of *Gulliver's Travels*. Three things about this volume must be said here. First, *A Tale of a Tub* is a satire with an explicitly Christian concern. It is a rigorously sceptical exploration of the historical corruption of belief and judgement by self-deception and self-interest. Affirming the location of truth outside as well as within the self, it recognizes in its very form and style the psychological difficulty inherent in the concepts of Reformation and Renaissance. It underlines the dilemmas inherent in belief and practice, but does not in principle deride Christian belief. Secondly, the innovative art of *A Tale of a Tub* lies in its relation of Narrative and Digressions, the latter probably composed later. It displays Swift's deliberate art of structuring his work through variation and contrast. Thirdly, the inset fable of the spider and the bee in *The Battle of the Books* affirms humanist values specifically relevant to *Gulliver's Travels*. The bee produces honey and wax, sweetness and light, from his travels over garden and meadow. By contrast the spider spins his web out of his own gut. This image of the spider, used by Bacon to deride reclusive medieval philosophy (*Advancement of Learning*, *Novum Organum*), is here applied to the would-be self-sufficient Modern Party in the current debates between Ancient and Modern learning. The bee is seen to be more genuinely creative. He is creative partly because of his mobility (travel and experience), partly because he can digest his experience, combining his own conclusions with what the world had revealed to him. Each of these points will be found to bear on *Gulliver's Travels*.

The next development in Swift's career raises the great issue of Party, the major new feature of the political life of his time.

Since the later seventeenth century two slang terms had arisen, one, 'Whig' from South-west Scotland, the other, 'Tory' from Ireland, and became the names of two broad areas of political opinion and practice. The very rise of these two insulting terms into public use suggests a new evolution in political life. Two things must be stressed here. First, Whig and Tory were terms with no precise or stable definition. Secondly, there was in Swift's time no acceptance of a two-party system resembling twentieth-century Democrats and Republicans in the USA or Conservative and Labour in Britain. While the terms were used seriously, indeed with passion, they were deployed by each side to attack the other as an enemy factor. Each side hoped to see the monarch guided by a circle of wise, experienced and orthodox councillors. Neither side believed Party to be other than a disease of the age. Largely owing to the events of 1688, the political world was irremediably entangled in a development of which it did not approve.

Once this is understood the political parties of Swift's earlier career may be roughly characterized. Whigs were happy to see William and Mary settled on the throne, supported the wars against France which William began, were ready to see change in the ancient constitution of the kingdoms, were inclined to tolerate Protestant but not Catholic dissent, and were to become associated with new financial developments emanating from the United Provinces, the founding of the Bank of England, the proliferation of joint stock companies, and wealth in stocks rather than land. Tories, though most of them opposed the Catholic measures of James II, distrusted William and Mary, and found it hard to deny the *de jure* claim to the throne of James II and his son. They increasingly opposed the huge military involvement on the continent, and increasingly felt the Church of England to be under threat from dissent and from secular attitudes. They distrusted wealth in stocks, and supported a landed interest on the ground that (as Swift himself put it in 1721): 'the possessors of the soil are the best judges of what is for the advantage of the kingdom' (*Correspondence*, II. 373).

Swift moved from the Whig to the Tory area of the political

arena in 1709–10 for a variety of reasons, public and personal. He did not feel that the Whig administrations adequately supported the Established Church, especially not in Ireland where it was needy and under threat. He became more and more alarmed at the length, scale and expense of the war with France, now being prosecuted under Queen Anne, and feared the ambition of Marlborough as Commander in Chief. What was more, Swift, though familiar with highly placed Whig politicians, had had no help from them for the Church in Ireland, and no significant promotion himself. As the Whig administration began to crumble in 1710, Swift let it be known that he felt himself ill-rewarded by the Whigs and, while he wished to keep in touch with them, might be willing to serve a government of a very different complexion. Robert Harley and Henry St John, the two rising Tory politicians, saw in Swift the skilled propagandist and powerful writer they needed to support their radically new, or radically old policies, above all their determination to bring to an end the apparently interminable war with France. In the eyes of the world Swift now changed his party. What the world saw was partly correct. But it may be noted that loyalty to the Church of England runs as a consistent motive through both Swift's Whig and Tory phases.

Brought in by a decision of Queen Anne, and with its less moderate elements strengthened by success in the General Election of 1710, the new administration established itself with Harley as Chancellor, and St John as Secretary for the Northern Department (thus responsible for any peace negotiations). Advised by Harley, the Queen acted on Swift's memorial in support of the Church in Ireland, where Swift's patron and friend the Duke of Ormonde now became Deputy. Swift anonymously wrote the periodical *The Examiner* (1710–11) in support of the government, whose great aim was now to end the war. In *The Conduct of the Allies* (1711) and *The Public Spirit of the Whigs* (1714) Swift produced the most powerful English prose in defence of a government since Milton. Samuel Johnson would write that Swift 'dictated for a time the political opinions of the English nation'. He also secured promotion: not the bishopric he certainly deserved but, after incredible complication, the Deanery of St Patrick's Cathedral, Dublin, in 1713. Meanwhile, in the realm of high politics, the long, complex negotiation of peace with France finally issued in the Treaty of Utrecht (1713): in the same year the Tories won even greater electoral success. But Harley was losing favour with the ailing Queen who also distrusted the rising ambition of St John. In her last act of state she appointed the Earl of Shewsbury, not St John, as Harley's successor. At her death on 1 August 1714 the influence of the Tories had thus been checked by the throne. Those who wanted a peaceful restoration of the House of Stuart never gained the initiative; the Whigs ensured, in the short term at least, a smooth transition to the House of Hanover and George I. For his part George felt the most rooted hostility to the Tories. On Hanoverian grounds he had favoured the war and regretted the peace. On dynastic grounds he rightly suspected the Tories of being more open to the idea of a Stuart restoration than the Whigs. At first it was apparent to the Tories that they had lost office. As time went by it became clear that they were proscribed. It was nearly half a century before they enjoyed office again.

Swift left England for his Irish deanery and took the Oaths to King George. He was nearly forty-seven. Having enjoyed a short period of influence and fame, he probably felt that the future held nothing in store save the conscientious discharge of his ecclesiastical office. At first, perhaps, Ireland seemed only the scene of his relative disappointment. Then, as he looked across at England and saw Harley imprisoned in the Tower, St John, Ormonde and, later, his friend Atterbury in exile and Jacobite service, he may have felt Ireland as safe a refuge from England as England had been from Ireland in 1689. Events and perspectives had changed, posing new problems of prudence and fidelity. For several years Swift engaged in no major literary work, though he worried away at political memoirs and wrote his *Enquiry into the Behaviour of the Queen's Last Ministry*. He obviously reviewed the political events of his life and this prompted him to think of history in a different way, with recognizable events and familiar forces transformed into a vision almost equally painful as comic. Part I of *Gulliver's Travels* was taking shape.

But before we first hear of the *Travels*, yet another view of Ireland had compelled Swift's attention. It was the most perennial view of all: Ireland as it was between the bloody collisions of high politics, an exploited colonial dependency rather than an equal kingdom of the British crown. Swift's engagement in the defence of Ireland's economic interests began with his publication in 1720 of his *Proposal for the Universal Use of Irish Manufacture*. Then in July 1722 Robert Walpole, leader of the new Whig administration at Westminster, sold a patent to one William Wood for the production of a debased copper currency for circulation in Ireland. Wood was thus favoured because Walpole was willing to ingratiate himself with the influential Duchess of Kendal, one of King George's mistresses, whom Wood had previously bribed. This edifying piece of statecraft enraged the whole Irish establishment, as much perhaps because of its insult to Ireland as its predicted threat to trade. Swift was encouraged to attack the measure, and did so by adopting the mask of M. B. Drapier, a fictional Dublin tradesman. His seven *Drapier's Letters* (1724–5) were so successful a challenge to the government that in August 1725 the patent was withdrawn. His part was not without danger (the government offered a reward for the discovery of the author), but he had Ireland behind him. Though his appeal was to Irish Protestants in the first place, the stand he took had implications for 'the Whole People of Ireland'. Swift's greatest and most famous Irish tract, *A Modest Proposal for Preventing the Children of Ireland From Being a Burden to their Parents Or Country* (1729), in which, in the character of a projector, he suggests the alleviation of poverty and starvation in Ireland by the killing and cooking of its young children ('whether Stewed, Roasted, Baked, or Boiled'), quite transcends religious distinction. No author has written so tellingly or memorably in the service of humanity.

On 15 April 1721, after the tract on *Irish Manufacture* and before the first *Drapier's Letter*, there occurs the first reference to *Gulliver's Travels*: 'I am now writing a History of my Travels, which will be a large Volume, and gives Account of Countryes hitherto unknown; but they go on slowly for want of Health and Humour' (*Correspondence*, II. 381).

The sources of *Gulliver's Travels* are literary, moral and psychological as well as historical. Yet it is clear that the historical and political events of Swift's lifetime too contribute to his book. The platitudes of history: the ingratitude and deceptions of princes, the conflicts of creed and party, the perils of power, unforeseen problems growing out of hard-won solutions, the lust for glory and the pursuit of interest − all this which can be rattled off without feeling had been perceived with feeling by Swift, often at first hand. The text of his *Travels* is so managed that their reader too is made to feel the experience behind the platitude. More than this, the shifting relation between England and Ireland within Swift's life not only revealed the volatility of distinct kingdoms, but powerfully underscored the baffling relation between location and viewpoint, different lands and different judgements.

Chapter 3

Marvels and voyages

As Swift worked on the first two books of *Gulliver's Travels* his friend Alexander Pope, having translated Homer's *Iliad*, proposed a new translation of the *Odyssey*, the first of all the voyage narratives of the marvellous. In Bk IX Odysseus and his crew are imprisoned by the one-eyed giant Polyphemus, the size of a mountain and with a voice like thunder. This barbarous shepherd eats several of Odysseus' seamen before the remainder manage to put out his eye with a stake and regain their ship. Even then the ship is nearly sunk as the giant flings rocks after them into the sea in his blind fury. Pope's wonderful translation of this episode may be compared with the terrifyingly factual manner with which Swift makes Gulliver tell how he is abandoned by his shipmates on the shore of Brobdingnag as 'a huge creature', a 'Monster', wades after their boat into the sea (I. 1). In the second century AD the *True History* of the Greek Lucian takes the marvellous voyage further into the fantastic, so much so as to achieve a satiric effect widely imitated in the Renaissance.

In the Christian Middle Ages the marvellous became the property of the romance, whether in verse or prose, whether narrative of land or sea. During the long European Renaissance the tale of the marvellous underwent more or less concurrently several overlapping or interlacing transformations. It could be made over into more explicit and systematic allegory in which (for example) giants, dragons and enchantments embodied moral or theological concepts, as in Spenser's *Faerie Queene* or Bunyan's *Pilgrim's Progress*. It could, retaining some of its original wonder, survive in the popular form of chapbook romance, stories meant for the relatively uneducated and for children. The end of this particular evolution might be found in Swift's *Tale of a Tub* where he tells how the brothers Peter,

Jack and Martin, in their early adventures, 'encountered a reasonable quantity of giants, and slew certain dragons'. This not only reveals Swift's fascination with popular story, but captures exactly the late Renaissance critical spirit as it plays upon romance. 'A reasonable quantity' bespeaks the world of judicious computation, while the word 'certain' prompts the gloomy recognition that though some dragons are killed others will always remain. Finally, as this example reminds us, the tale of the marvellous could be assimilated into the prose of humanist comedy. Three years after the publication of *Gulliver's Travels* Pope was to praise Swift,

> Whether thou chuse Cervantes' serious air,
> Or laugh and shake in Rab'lais' easy Chair ...
> *(The Dunciad*, I. 19–20)

and thus compare Swift with two of the greatest Renaissance authors of this formal and intellectual conversion of marvel into comedy. Each in his own way was a master of the mental vision, each a master of the solidity and energies of the physical world, and of the improbable ways in which the physical and visionary could mingle. In Rabelais' *Gargantua and Pantagruel* the giant Gargantua accidentally ate six pilgrims in the lettuce of his salad, but they, clinging perilously to his teeth as he swallowed a great draught of wine, were eventually plucked out with his tooth-pick, and pissed away across the countryside in a torrent of his urine (I. xxxviii). This is one of the Renaissance ways with the marvellous. Less different from Homer's Polyphemus episode than one might think − each is realized in full physical detail, each can imagine how a giant feels as well as a man − Rabelais uses the marvellous to a festively comic end. Gargantua does not mean to consume the pilgrims, who all eventually escape, and he does not suffer like Polyphemus. The pilgrims suffer greater comic humiliation than Odysseus' crew, for it is more ignominious to be ejected from prison with a tooth pick than escape clinging beneath a sheep or a ram. The physical life of Rabelais' giant may be dangerous to ordinary human beings, but it is neither terrible nor shameful. Indeed Rabelais looks at physical life in a new way, and the

sense of unconstrained laughter at his physical fantasy –
'laugh and shake' as Pope puts it – is appropriate to its
uninhibited satisfaction in bodily life. Swift, 'a great reader and
admirer of Rabelais' (Spence, p. 133), who praised Cervantes
and Rabelais for their 'true humour' (*Intelligencer*, III; *Works*,
xii.32; also III. 381), will be seen to build on and transform
the Rabelaisian situation. As we shall see, comedy, both physical
and mental, is the very medium in which Swift launches his
ideas.

The last two books of *Gargantua and Pantagruel*, (Bk V not,
perhaps, by Rabelais) were translated during Swift's early life
by Peter Motteux, and comprise a voyage to the Oracle of the
Holy Bottle. More, perhaps, than the earlier books, these are
what Motteux termed 'satirical allegories', and he appended
his own explanations of all the islands and episodes of this
imaginary voyage. Two other works claim attention here:
Joseph Hall's *Mundus Alter et Idem* (published in Latin in
1605; translated into English 1609) and Cyrano de Bergerac's
Histoire Comique de la Lune (1657), each generally influenced
by Rabelais. In the first Mercurius Brittanicus sails in his ship
Phantasia to *four* imaginary countries, Crapulia, Viraginia,
Moronia and Lavernia, lands of gluttony, women, folly and
deceit (McCabe, *Joseph Hall*, p. 74). A plausible-looking map
is included. In the *Histoire Comique* Cyrano visits giants and
a dwarf on the moon (Turner, p. xvi).

Overlapping in some measure with such comic represen-
tations of the marvellous are imaginary voyages of a rather
different kind. Pre-eminent among these, and certain to have
been known to Swift, is the *Utopia* of that same Sir Thomas
More who is listed with Socrates, Epaminondas, and three
Roman exemplars of republican liberty, in Part III of *Gulliver's
Travels*, as 'A Sextumvirate to which all the Ages of the World
cannot add a Seventh' (III. vii. 196). More's work is of the
first relevance to *Gulliver's Travels*, and several features of it
must be mentioned here. *Utopia* consists of two books of
which the second describes an ideal commonwealth: ideal in
the sense of being, in fact, imaginary; ideal too in the sense
that the sunburnt voyager in More's fiction who describes it

judges it to be a perfect commonwealth. The true title of More's work is, in fact, *Concerning the Best State of a Commonwealth* though, as will be seen, this does not necessarily endorse the voyager's view. The name given to this commonwealth, 'Utopia', means literally 'no place' in Greek, while the name of the voyager is Hythodaeus or Hythloday, 'expert in nonsense', 'visionary' (Baker-Smith, *More and Plato's Voyage*, pp. 13–14). Further, Bk I of *Utopia*, which describes the condition of England in More's time, was written later, partly to give a strong contrast between Utopia and contemporary reality, partly to supply a framework of dialogue for Hythloday's account. The total text of *Utopia* thus contains a variety of opinions, important in which are not only those of Hythloday, but those of Morus, More's own *persona* within his work, whose name also lent itself to wordplay on *moria*, Greek for folly. Morus does not fully share the enthusiasm of Hythloday for the commonwealth of the Utopians. As he makes clear towards the end of Bk I, he does not endorse the latter's all-or-nothing attitude to the adoption of the Utopian model, preferring piecemeal reform where opportunity offers. His concluding words, at the end of Bk II, accurately convey his modest and circumspect assessment:

In the mean time, as I can not agree and consent to all thinges that he said, being else without dowte a man singularly well learned, and also in all wordely matters exactely and profoundely experienced, so must I needes confesse and graunt, that many thinges be in the Vtopian weal-publique which in our cities I may rather wishe for then hoope after'   (Robinson translation, pp. 308–9).

Two points in particular bear upon Swift. First, an ideal commonwealth may be set forth less for unanimous approval than the provocation of discussion and thought. Secondly, the careful poising of these different attitudes, desire for Utopia, distrust of Utopia, is the outcome of the total structure of the work, its two books not just being in loose succession but necessary to one another in a creative dialogue.

The era connecting More and Swift saw the production of many other Utopias, some of the more notable such as Francis Bacon's *New Atlantis*, presented through the convention of the imaginary voyage. These in themselves were numerous enough to establish a genre and thus a pattern of expectation in any reader who picked up such a book. In her major study *Swift and the Age of Compromise* Kathleen Williams considered some of these in relation to Swift, works which set out to show what a purely rationalistic society might be like. Among them are Gabriel de Foigny's *La Terre Australe Connue* (1676; translated into English 1693) and Denis Vairasse d'Allais' *Histoire de Sévarambes* (1677–9) which sufficiently resembled *Gulliver's Travels* at first glance to be added to it as a spurious third volume in 1727 by an unscrupulous bookseller.

Writers of the serious imaginary voyage studied the appearance of probability. More made Hythloday a Portuguese and thus a countryman of the great voyager Vasco da Gama; he also made him a companion and fellow-voyager of Amerigo Vespucci, the discoverer after whom America was named. Utopia was thus associated in More's fiction with real explorers and real discoverers. A demand for verisimilitude naturally focused on the changing idiom of non-fictional maritime narratives, which were plentiful in the sixteenth, seventeenth and eighteenth centuries. The two great publishers of voyages, Richard Hakluyt and Samuel Purchas, included in their huge compilations materials of diverse kinds, but it is worth noting the differing attitude to voyages of the collectors themselves. In his *Principal Navigations, Voyages, Traffics and Discoveries of the English Nation* (1589–1600) Hakluyt's concern is historical and practical, economic and national: voyages afforded essential geographical evidence in a projected enterprise of world-wide trade and settlement. Purchas, on the other hand, in his three books, *Purchas His Pilgrimage* (1613), *Purchas His Pilgrim* (1619) and *Purchas His Pilgrims* (1625) adopts an explicitly religious attitude to voyages, and sets forth an allegorical mode of reading voyage narratives based on interpretation of Holy Scripture. Voyages to him could be allegories of the journey of the Christian soul to is haven in heaven. For him Solmon's navy prefigured the Church Militant, the sea the world, the wind the Holy Spirit, while 'Christ himselfe' was 'the Load-starre and Sunne of Truth' (*Purchas His Pilgrims*,

p. 3). This way of thinking about sea voyages was popular and lasting, as the numerous editions of John Flavell's *Navigation Spiritualised* ... (?1682) demonstrate. His book went on being published in different versions throughout the next century.

Very different in approach was one of the most important voyage narratives to be published during Swift's earlier life: the pirate William Dampier's *New Voyage Round the World* (1697). This is the book by 'My Cousin Dampier' specifically mentioned in the 'Letter from Capt. Gulliver to His Cousin Sympson' which was added to *Gulliver's Travels* in 1735. Swift there hints that *A New Voyage* was revised by a young gentleman of a university; certainly Dampier's narrative is well-written in a clear, close and factual style of the most modern kind. Its style is worth attention, for Dampier's book was certainly one of Swift's most important models for the *Travels*. Dampier's modern idiom stemmed from the marriage of colloquial speech with the Renaissance imitation of Seneca and Tacitus, Latin models of brevity and telling plainness. Familiarized into a variety of English writing, it grew flexible, seemed 'natural', and was favoured by Royal Society propagandists in the later seventeenth century as the most truthful language a writer could use. It became a form of realism, and sought by its very plainness to reach a general reader. Dampier's narrative avoids 'tarpaulin' – a prevalence of nautical language – and seems addressed to a polite and educated readership. 'I have frequently indeed divested myself of Sea-Phrases, to gratify the Land Reader; for which the Seamen will hardly forgive me' (Preface, A3ᵛ). Dedicated to Charles Mountagu, President of the Royal Society, and supplied with reliable maps, together with some representation of 'Terra Australis Incognita', Dampier's book appeals to a concern with the practical and useful within the expanding realm of Natural Philosophy. In keeping with these features, it is sometimes suggested that Dampier is a wholly secular writer. But this is not the case. While Dampier's tone is certainly not generally religious, at times of particular peril or deliverance, both in *A New Voyage* and in *A Voyage to New Holland* (1699), there are passages of religious reflection such as the following:

The evening of this 18th day was very dismal. The Sky looked very black, being covered with dark Clouds, the Wind blew hard, and the Seas ran high. The Sea was already roaring in a white foame about us; a dark night coming on, and no Land in sight to shelter us, and our little Ark in danger to be swallowed by every Wave; and what was worst of all, none of us thought ourselves prepared for another World.

... I made very sad reflections on my former Life, and lookt back with horror and detestation, on actions which before I disliked, but now I trembled at the remembrance of ... I did also call to mind the many miraculous acts of God's Providence towards me, in the whole course of my life, of which kind, I believe few men met the like. For all these I returned thanks in a peculiar manner, and this once more desired Gods assistance, and composed my mind, as well as I could, in the hopes of it, and, as the event shew'd, I was not disappointed of my hopes.

(*A New Voyage*, pp. 496–7; collated with Swift's copy, 3rd edn, 1698)

Thus, in a storm off the coast of Sumatra, Dampier and his companions submitted themselves to 'God's good providence'.

Swift had in his library an edition of Hakluyt's *Principal Navigations*, *Purchas His Pilgrims*, and Dampier's *New Voyage* (*Works*, XI. xiv). It is probable that he read or re-read them at the time when he was thinking of *Gulliver* and reading 'I know not how many diverting books of history and travels' (*Correspondence*, III. 134). Landmarks among this wider reading, they suggest that there was nothing inevitable in Swift's conception of *Gulliver's Travels*. Taking his cue from Hakluyt his approach to the writing of fictional voyages might have been strongly patriotic. It would then have accorded with the maritime and imperial expansion of eighteenth-century Britain. In view of the Christian themes of *A Tale of a Tub* he might, prompted by Purchas, have produced a Christian allegory, part satirical, part pious. Dampier supplied him with the newest model, and is the one he came closest to adopting. But if we see Dampier constituting the norm for eighteenth-century voyage-writing, we have to acknowledge that rare but significant passages of religious emotion are included in his example. Yet it is precisely in this respect that the Dean departs from the precedent of the pirate. I shall return to this point in future chapters.

If we put together in our mind a real voyager like Dampier and an imaginary voyager such as Hythloday, we shall see that there was a further reason why readers in Swift's time were interested in voyages and travels. Improbable as it may seem, such narratives sometimes appeared likely to settle current questions in political theory. The great question: What was the origin of government? has been invoked from the sixteenth century on as a guide to or (more often) retrospective justification of political conduct. The patriarchal doctrine that humankind had lived under government since the paternal kingship of Adam was deployed, in the seventeenth century, in support of the traditional and legitimate Stuart monarchy. The contrary hypothesis, that man had been born in a state of nature, and that if government had been subsequently established this must have been by original contract, by which the weaker yielded some of their freedom to the stronger in return for protection, was used to argue that kings and other rulers might be deposed for violation of that contract. Such was John Locke's position in his *Two Treatises of Government*. This book was composed before the 1688 Revolution which drove away King James and accepted William and Mary, published just after, in 1689, and later revised and republished in 1698. Travel narratives might reveal new societies with different or confirming myths of the origin of government. For example, in his ch. xii Dampier describes the 'Civil State of the Isle of Mandanao' (3rd edn, p. 324). Further, they might possibly discover a people still living in a state of nature, or at least examples of individuals in the natural state. In pursuit of such examples Locke mentions binding, non-political compacts between 'two men in Soldania' (Saldanha Bay in South Africa) and 'the two Men in the Desert Island, mentioned by Garcilasso De la Vega in his History of *Peru*, or between a *Swiss* and an *Indian*, in the Woods of *America* ... though perfectly in a State of Nature ...' (Second Treatise, II. 14; ed. Laslett, pp. 317–18). Far from articulating the political orthodoxy of a new age (as used to be thought) Locke's *Two Treatises* was among the most divisive works of political theory in Swift's lifetime (Dunn, *The Political Thought of Locke*; Kenyon,

Revolution Principles). The potential relevance of strange lands and new peoples to Locke's still controversial hypothesis of government was great, and we might expect the writers of imaginary voyages to play on such expectation. Locke's mention of 'two Men in the Desert Island' brings to mind one last book which strongly invites comparison with *Gulliver's Travels*. This is Daniel Defoe's *The Life and Strange Surprising Adventures of Robinson Crusoe, of York, Mariner ... Written by Himself* (1719). There is no evidence that Swift read *Robinson Crusoe*, yet he seems to have known of Defoe as a controversialist during the two previous reigns, and it is probably significant that *Crusoe* was published just as (or perhaps very shortly before) Swift was beginning to conceive his own new book. It has been said that *Gulliver* 'starts like a novel' (Turner, p. xv); it certainly starts like *Crusoe*:

I was born in the Year 1632, in the City of *York*, of a good Family, tho' not of that Country; my Father being a Foreigner of *Bremen*, who first settled at *Hull* ...   (*Crusoe*, ed. Crowley, p. 3)
My Father had a small Estate in *Nottinghamshire*; I was the Third of five Sons. He sent me to *Emanuel-College*, in *Cambridge*, at Fourteen Years old, where I resided three Years ...   (*Gulliver*, ed. Turner, p. 3)

The method is the same though the details differ. In each case the narrator is authenticated by a plain statement of his origin: plausible social circumstance links the writer to known places and institutions, and extends to include his early economic situation. In each case the detail is suggestive. Crusoe's family derives from Protestant northern Europe (like William III and George I). Gulliver is something of a university man, from a Cambridge College of Puritan foundation (it had been Joseph Hall's College).

    Robinson Crusoe throws into high relief a feature of *Gulliver's Travels* already touched on: its paucity in Christian reference and religious emotion. Defoe's text is, by comparison, saturated in the conviction of a Christian providence:

I was now landed, and safe on Shore, and began to look up and thank God that my Life was sav'd in a Case wherein there was some Minutes before scarce any room to hope.   (p. 46)

Thus Defoe recounts one of the most potentially religious moments in a mariner's experience: safe landfall after the dangers of shipwreck. As Crusoe begins to re-make his life on his solitary and desert island, he finds one day 'ten or twelve Ears' of 'our *English* Barley' (or very like) springing from the soil:

It is impossible to express the Astonishment and Confusion of my Thoughts on this Occasion; I had hitherto acted on no religious Foundation at all, indeed I had very few Notions of Religion in my Head, or had entertain'd any Sense of any Thing that had befallen me, otherwise than as a Chance, or, as we lightly say, what pleases God; without so much as enquiring into the End of Providence in these Things, or his Order in governing Events in the World: But after I saw Barley grow there, in a Climate which I knew was not proper for Corn, and especially that I knew not how it came there, it startl'd me strangely, and I began to suggest, that God had miraculously caus'd this Grain to grow without any help of Seed sown, and that it was so directed purely for my Sustenance, on that wild miserable Place.

This touch'd my Heart a little, and brought Tears out of my Eyes, and I began to bless myself ... (p. 78)

This is far from the idiom of *Gulliver*, though it has precedent in Dampier. If Dampier be posited as a norm, then the fervent religious expression of *Crusoe* is as clearly on one side of this norm as the religious reticence of *Gulliver* is on the other.

Still more obvious is the difference between Defoe's story of how a shipwrecked mariner prospers on an uninhabited island, and Swift's stories of how a shipwrecked or abandoned mariner encounters four firmly established, if wonderfully strange, communities of intelligent beings. In his isolation, on what seems 'the *Island of Despair*' (p. 70), Crusoe replicates what Defoe considered the supreme rôle within his native kingdom, and becomes the providential monarch of a new community (Schonhorn, *Defoe's Politics*, ch. 6). If we compare Locke's 'two Men in the Desert Island' with Defoe's, we see that the novelist has not shown us two men in a state of nature. Crusoe is already providential lord of the island. The first encounter of Crusoe and Friday is nevertheless a Lockeian moment, for the savage, 'seeing himself a little at Liberty, Nature inspir'd him with Hopes of Life' (p. 201), and Crusoe demonstrated his capacity to save him from his pursuers. Man Friday then swears

to be his slave for ever, though he actually becomes a subject and
servant. An 'original contract' has in the urgency of the crisis
taken place: Friday will obey Crusoe, Crusoe will protect Friday.
Defoe fills the human space of Crusoe's island with the dynamic
which brought William as deliverer monarch to England before
the end of Crusoe's lifetime, and which Defoe may have felt had
brought the House of Brunswick to the throne on the death of
Anne. Swift, by contrast, plays the game of discovering, re-
acting, learning and judging. Gulliver (whose first name,
Lemuel, is that of an obscure Hebrew king) is never in the
position of a king in *Gulliver's Travels*.

It will nevertheless be found that Gulliver is more than a
mere reporter of other societies. This is the rôle of Hythloday
in regard to the Utopians, and he comes to life chiefly in relation
to Morus and other non-Utopians in More's text. Swift is at
pains to confront Gulliver with difficult decisions in most of
the strange lands he visits, so that in a way his rôle is dynamic,
though often not admirable, in relation to the communities he
encounters. Under the providence of God, Crusoe is active
from the start. Gulliver is always initially the observer, and is
thereafter reactive: the parts he plays move towards moral
judgements which, to a decreasing degree, are expressed through
physical action.

The two different books of More's text set forth two different
commonwealths: Bk I the kingdom of England in its setting of
Renaissance Europe, Bk II the commonwealth of the Utopians.
Different communities become different books. As Swift read
through voyages real and imaginary, ancient and modern, in
preparation for writing *Gulliver's Travels*, his own strange
experience of different kingdoms must have prompted him to
write, not a single seamless narrative of imaginary travel, but a
story heavily punctuated into four separate Parts, four separate
commonwealths, something like the four separate countries of
Joseph Hall's *Mundus Alter et Idem*, and recalling, perhaps,
the four voyages of Amerigo Vespucci mentioned by Morus at
the beginning of *Utopia*.

Chapter 4

A voyage to Lilliput

Lemuel Gulliver presents himself to the reader as an educated man (he has studied at Cambridge and Leyden) but of small fortune and no worldly success. He is in fact educated above his station. Apprenticed to a surgeon, he makes several unprofitable voyages, marries, practises as a physician, fails, goes to sea again, as ship's surgeon, again attempts to settle down and practise as a doctor but again fails to thrive, and eventually accepts an offer to sail in the Antelope with Captain William Pritchard to 'the *South-Sea*' (I.i.3−4). After the bursting of the South Sea Bubble in 1721 this particular wording sounds a faint but clear note of warning.

This voyage is at first 'prosperous', until a storm drives the Antelope onto a rock off the coast of Van Dieman's Land (part of Terra Australis Incognita). In the plain, practical English of Dampier or Defoe, and in a paragraph of inordinate length, Gulliver narrates his attempt to reach land in one of the ship's boats with six other members of the crew. They row until they are exhausted and must trust themselves 'to the Mercy of the Waves'. The boat is then overturned by the wind, and Gulliver swims 'as Fortune directed me ... pushed forward by Wind and Tide' (I.i.5). He just manages to reach land and, from the physical struggle and the brandy he has drunk before leaving the ship, falls into a long and deep slumber. The reader notices that it is to the mercy of the waves only that Gulliver says he has entrusted himself, and that he has swum as Fortune, not Providence, directed.

Still in the same long paragraph Gulliver awakes at dawn unable to stir. His whole body is fastened to the ground, even his hair. He can only see the sky. But very gradually, aware of something alive moving over him, he is able to perceive 'a human creature not six Inches high, with a Bow and Arrow in his Hands, and a Quiver at his Back' (I.i.6), walking up his chest. The narrative carries steadily on in its plain, physical and circumstantial manner, with two further references to 'Fortune' (I.i.6,7) and the end of it all is that Gulliver has become the captive of a midget people, speaking their own language, and commanded for the moment by a *Hurgo*, or 'great Lord' (I.i.8).

This is the first great metamorphosis of *Gulliver's Travels*. In a totally clear, professional, Dampier-like style, Gulliver's tale has taken us beyond the pigmies sometimes plausibly referred to in voyage narratives into the realm of romance, of fairy-land. Swift's prose style has everything to do with the achievement of this transition. It is a style which offers itself as a clear medium through which to see the world. As it is handled here almost every clause seems to constitute a new perception or calculation. These clauses, most of which could easily become that most basic unit of prose the simple sentence, are never here allowed to gain momentum or build up into a climax. We may feel that the natural climax of the narrative is the moment when Gulliver wakes up to find himself fixed to the ground while the midget archer advances up his chest. This marvel, which in other hands might have occasioned bold metaphor and exclamation, is, as it were, ignored by a journal-like style apparently absorbed in the accumulation of exact particulars. These particulars actually build up a situation within which we feel Gulliver's latent fear in the face of a sudden and inexplicable physical constraint. But this is not Kafka's *Metamorphosis*: as soon as the tiny archer comes into view, Gulliver's attention, and the reader's with it, is directed to these little people, so intrepid and resourceful, with whom it seems communication and bargain may be possible. The reader is in a world of wonders like that of Rabelais, save that in Rabelais we witnessed giants and men mingling together, while here it is only our countryman, the ship's surgeon from Emmanuel College and Wapping, who (we gradually realize) is Gargantuan, while all the rest are midgets. Swift has 'methodized' Rabelais' copious comic epic of the human and the gigantic, with definite consequences for the reader's viewpoint. We continue to see the world through Gulliver's eyes but, as the narrative proceeds, our own curiosity to see a giant at close quarters gives us a special sympathy with Lilliputian reaction: when Gulliver roars with astonishment, they hurl themselves off his body in terror (a most Rabelaisian moment) but soon return. This desire in the reader to contemplate the gigantic at length and in full will not be satisfied until Part II. Meanwhile Swift's immense paragraph, so necessary if continuity of form is to negotiate plausibly such an amazing transition, reaches its conclusion with the information that the resourceful Emperor of Lilliput has had a sleeping potion put in Gulliver's wine.

Gulliver's Travels has perhaps suffered from the fact that in all the libraries of commentary on it so much space has been devoted to the attempt to interpret Swift's meaning. While he certainly intended to puzzle and vex those who sought in his book a moral as plain as his English, interpretation is not the only task that a responsible criticism of *Gulliver* should undertake. Appreciation of the fiction is just as important. In 'A Voyage to Lilliput', for example, what chiefly strikes the reader is the inventiveness of the narrative, and the sheer imaginative ingenuity with which Swift's intelligence plays upon the different scales of physical life. Lilliput has the character of a beautifully made toy world (Gulliver later speaks of dolls' houses in London toy shops – II. iii. 97) and every detail is considered and crafted to perfection. These features no doubt account for the enduring life of *Gulliver's Travels* as a children's book (see Endnote), and its eighteenth-century existence in abbreviated popular form (Rogers, pp. 178–81). Swift's narrative blurs nothing, but brings its impossible experience to life in the most fresh, exact and plausible way. Thus the shower of arrows shot into Gulliver's body by the Lilliputians 'pricked me like so many Needles' (II. i. 6): small but exceedingly painful. When Gulliver has the chance to make water, 'which I very plentifully did', the Lilliputians, conjecturing what he was going to do, 'opened to the right and left ... to avoid the Torrent' (I. i. 10) and thus avoided the misfortune of the pilgrims in Rabelais. Later, when an inventory is made of the objects in his pockets, his watch is described with all the freshness of intelligent ignorance:

'a Globe, half Silver, and half of some transparent Metal: for on the transparent Side we saw certain strange Figures circularly drawn, and thought we could touch them, until we found our Fingers stopped with that lucid Substance. He put this Engine to our Ears, which made an incessant Noise like that of a Water-Mill. And we conjecture it is either some unknown Animal, or the God that he worships ...' (I.ii.21).

After Gulliver has been transported to the capital city of Lilliput, and signed the Articles with the Emperor which granted him liberty on conditions, the Emperor is eager to show Gulliver the magnificence of the imperial palace:

But this [seeing the palace] I was not able to do till three Days after, which I spent in cutting down with my Knife some of the largest Trees in the Royal Park, about an Hundred Yards distant from the City. Of these Trees I made two Stools, each about three Foot high, and strong enough to bear my Weight. The People having received Notice a second time, I went again through the City to the Palace, with my two Stools in my Hands. When I came to the Side of the outer Court, I stood upon on Stool, and took the other in my Hand: This I lifted over the Roof, and gently set it down on the Space between the first and second Court, which was eight Foot wide. I then stept over the Buildings very conveniently from one Stool to the other, and drew up the first after me with a hooked Stick. By this Contrivance I got into the inmost Court; and lying down upon my Side, I applied my Face to the Windows of the middle Stories, which were left open on Purpose, and discovered the most splendid Apartments that can be imagined. There I saw the Empress, and the young Princes in their several Lodgings, with their chief Attendants about them. Her Imperial Majesty was pleased to smile very graciously upon me, and gave me out of the Window her Hand to kiss.   (I.iv.33)

This exemplifies important qualities, not only in the first two books of the *Travels* where physical scale is so important, but in the work as a whole. The emphasis is on 'Contrivance': how physical difficulties can be solved. Here the problem is how the giant Gulliver can get into the inmost court of the tiny fragile imperial palace without knocking down and destroying something. The details are carefully worked out, and it is typical of Swift that he considers the difficulty of retrieving the first stool from an acutely circumscribed position and thus specifies that useful object, 'a hooked Stick'. We see too that

here Gulliver's account is climactic: all the careful preparation
(clause by clause) finally gets him into the inmost sanctuary,
where not only does he see 'the most splendid Apartments' (we
note the unusual perception and diction), but her Imperial
Majesty smiles upon him and actually gives him her hand to
kiss. Gulliver could hardly have been more fortunate and
successful.

Swift's remarkable physical contrivance of his fictional
worlds ought not to be neglected because, apart from the
simple pleasure we may feel at his joining of the wonderful
and the practical, these worlds are the necessary basis for the
building of the reader's viewpoint. A childlike delight at the
Lilliputians and their world ('The Country round appeared
like a continued Garden ...') leads us into a natural concurrence
with Gulliver's gentle treatment of them. At an early point it
occurs to him to act like an angry Polyphemus and, seizing
forty or fifty Lilliputians as they passed over his body, 'dash
them against the Ground' (I. i. 8), but considerations of honour
and decency prevent him. He has, after all, given his word
to be submissive, while the little people are feeding him, at
presumably enormous expense, with adequate amounts of
food and drink. A little while later some Lilliputians nearly
put out his eye with an arrow (a premonition of things to
come) are are delivered up to him for punishment. After
pretending to prepare to eat them, Gulliver lets them go, and
wins golden opinions 'at this Mark of my Clemency' (I. ii. 17).
Like a liberal-minded anthropologist, Gulliver accepts the
ways of Lilliput and conforms as far as it is practicable for
him to do. He observes the significance of their titles and
distinctions and when, after signal service to the state, the
Emperor creates him a *Nardac*, 'which is the highest Title of
Honour among them' (I. v. 39), there can be no doubt that he
is gratified. As Lilliput opens out before us and takes Gulliver
in, the reader slides into accepting his acquiescence. For a long
time nothing happens to challenge this attitude, though Swift
works in such a way as implicitly to lay by a good deal of
significant evidence. For example, in the above account of
Gulliver's visit to court, are we amused at the use of two stools

to get into the imperial presence, and do we wonder what would have happened if Gulliver had fallen between them? Does it say anything about all that splendour that one has to lie flat on the ground and on one side to witness it? Is Gulliver naive to take Lilliput so seriously and would we think better of him had he been invited to court by an emperor his own size?

Some of these questions turn on what might be called the Utopian issue. What sort of Nowhere society is Lilliput? The reader has perhaps been sufficiently beguiled by Gulliver's plausible narrative of his impossible adventures that he has thought little about the highly centralized and enterprising society in which he finds himself, with its rich agriculture, its brave soldiers, its great lords, its emperor, its rabble, and the huge deconsecrated temple which serves as a 'spacious kennel' for the originally enchained narrator. These details alone, collected from the earlier narrative, sketch a pretty familiar society. When Gulliver writes that the Emperor has an '*Austrian* (that is a Habsburg) Lip' (I. ii. 15) the suspicion is confirmed that Lilliput, far from being like the common-wealth of the Utopians, rather resembles a late Renaissance monarchy. All this is confirmed by several connected accounts of Lilliputian social and political life, often associated with information from Gulliver's 'Friend *Reldresal*, principal Sec-retary for private Affairs' (I. iii. 25). The public rope dance for promotion to high office, and the capacity of '*Flimnap*, the Treasurer' to cut a higher caper on the 'strait Rope' than any other lord in the empire, and even to turn a somersault on it, are here mentioned. The significance hardly needs to be under-lined; it needs only to be added that Flimnap's skill is typical of the quick cleverness of the Lilliputians. In the same style is the '*leaping* and *creeping*' ceremony undergone by Lilliputians who are candidates for decorations of honour (I. iii. 26).

Such practices as these do not redound to the credit of Lilliput, and make in an amusing way a somewhat standard judgement on the behaviour of all those who compete in society for high office and honour. However, the historical and political account of Lilliput given by Reldresal to Gulliver in chapter 4, soon after the latter's visit to court, takes the presentation of Lilliput a long stage further. The function of this discourse is to gather together and reinforce much that the reader may have incidentally noted during Gulliver's narrative of his arrival and reception in the land of the little people. Here for the first time we are given a political diagnosis:

For, *said he*, as flourishing a Condition as we appear to be in to Foreigners, we labour under two mighty Evils; a violent Faction at Home, and the Danger of an Invasion by a most potent Enemy from abroad. As to the first, you are to understand, that for above seventy Moons past, there have been two struggling Parties in this Empire, under the Names of *Tramecksan*, and *Slamecksan*, from the high and low Heels on their Shoes, by which they distinguish themselves.

(I. iv. 34)

Reldresal proceeds to note that while the High Heels are closest to the 'ancient Constitution' and more numerous, the Emperor has resolved to employ only Low Heels in his Administration, that the 'Heir to the Crown' seems to have *some* tendency to the High Heels, hence the 'Hobble in his Gait', and that the great neighbouring Empire of Blefuscu is about to take advantage of 'these intestine Disquiets' in Lilliput to invade. As soon as Reldresal mentions factions and parties it is clear that Swift, through Gulliver's narrative, is doing more than convey standard satire of princes and ministers. It is all starting to sound like the history of England in Swift's time, and even more so as it goes on. There has been, we learn with Gulliver, 'a most obstinate War' between Lilliput and Blefuscu for 'six and thirty Moons past':

It began upon the following Occasion. It is allowed on all Hands, that the primitive Way of breaking Eggs before we eat them, was upon the larger End: But his present Majesty's Grand-father, while he was a Boy, going to eat an Egg, and breaking it according to the ancient Practice, happened to cut one of his Fingers. Whereupon the Emperor, his Father, published an Edict, commanding all his Subjects, upon great Penalties, to break the smaller End of their Eggs. The People have so highly resented this Law, that our Histories tell us, there have been six Rebellions raised on that Account; wherein one Emperor lost his Life, and another his Crown. These civil Commotions were constantly fomented by the Monarchs of *Blefuscu*;

and when they were quelled, the Exiles always fled for Refuge to that Empire. It is computed, that eleven Thousand Persons have, at several Times, suffered Death, rather than submit to break their Eggs at the smaller End. Many Hundred large Volumes have been published upon this Controversy: But the Books of the *Big-Endians* have been long forbidden, and the whole Party rendred incapable by Law of holding Employments.   (I. iv. 35–6)

Reldresal concludes his discourse by recalling the Articles of agreement signed between the Emperor and Gulliver, and informing him that, in the present danger of invasion from Blefuscu, 'his Imperial Majesty, placing great Confidence in your Valour and Strength, hath commanded me to lay this Account of his Affairs before you' (I. iv. 36).

The discourse of Secretary Reldresal is not only a prelude to dramatic action by Gulliver, but could have been thought by Swift's readers in 1726 to refer to the history of one country, and one country alone: it could only be England. Only England was a monarchy with parties or factions developed to this degree, and with the more numerous and traditional party currently proscribed from office. Only England had had one monarch who lost his life (Charles I) and another his crown (James II) within recent memory. As for the 'obstinate War', the long wars between Britain and France which were such a feature of Swift's world as a younger man, the War of the League of Augsburg 1689–97 and the War of the Spanish Succession 1701–13, are certainly meant. Though many other nations engaged in this protracted conflict, the allusion to Blefuscu exploiting the party divisions of Lilliput as France did those of Britain fixes the reference. It should, however, be appreciated that particular contemporary allusion does not rule out general allusion. Swift well knew that long wars and civil dissensions were, if not exactly timeless, pretty recurrent features in the history of states. What he gives us here, through Reldresal's discourse to Gulliver, is generalization sharpened by particularity. No reader in 1726 could not have thought about Whigs and Tories, England and France, when Slamecksan and Tramecksan, Lilliput and Blefuscu, came up at this point in the text.

Something subtler is effected with the account of Big-Endians and Little-Endians, sometimes glossed as an allusion to Catholic and Protestant. Charles I did not lose his life for the *Catholic* cause (he was a Protestant) though James II lost his throne for it. Yet it is clear that this division is more profound than that of party, for its consequences are more dire. Further, the egg, a common form of food, has also been held an emblem of the Holy Eucharist: this conflict, then, is probably one of religion, and 'Big-Endian' seems to convey doctrines which derive authority from divinity, while 'Little-Endian' would derive it from man.

All this talk of eggs and shoes, of course, belittles the formidable divisions between man and man in a way similar to that of Swift's earlier *Tale of a Tub*. It does so at that point in Part I when the strange, miniature world of Lilliput is quite suddenly revealed as something like a mirror-image of Swift's own and his readers' world, in its recent history. Swift's book either says that all these conflicts are really as trivial as eggs and heels and the pretensions of midgets (a healthy dose of coarse mockery against human values), or it says that human-kind makes itself morally small by treating such important divisions as though they were all physical and trivial. On the face of it, Swift gains satiric advantage from each alternative because on the face of it the reader does not work out their incompatibility. On deeper analysis it may seem that it is not wrong to take a side in such apparently small or mistaken conflicts: Gulliver as he now starts to emerge may be naive, but is hardly foolish or vicious. There is some resemblance here to the preoccupation of More/Morus in *Utopia* with whether or not to play an important part in a very un-Utopian world.

At this point in Part I it is clear that Swift has executed a twofold, strategic joke. First, the imperturbable modern Dampier-like narrative lands us in a kind of Rabelaisian wonder-land. Then, when we are prepared to read what must obviously be a fictional commonwealth as one provocatively and valuably different from our own, it becomes clear that this little fictional world is just like our own large factual one. So much for

Locke's interest in travellers' narratives as revealing peoples in a state of nature, or the origin of government in original contract! We look, comfortably enough, for profitable lessons from a strange and remote commonwealth, and find in it only our own selves and our own society.

Reldresal's discourse issues immediately in Gulliver's resolve to honour the agreement he has signed with the Emperor and involve himself in the impending international crisis between Lilliput and Blefuscu. Discourse now turns to narrative as Gulliver resolves to capture the enemy fleet. Carrying some packthread and a large number of knitting needles he wades and swims the channel between Lilliput and Blefuscu, which was at high water 'seventy *Glumgluffs* deep, which is about six Foot' (I. v. 37). He makes fast the enemy fleet but, as before, is terribly vulnerable to being blinded by arrows, until it occurs to him to protect his eyes with his spectacles, which he had managed to conceal during the earlier search of his pockets. A tense moment ensues. The Blefuscudians, who expect him merely to cut their ships adrift to run foul on each other, when they see Gulliver drawing away their fleet 'set up such a Scream of Grief and Dispair, that it is impossible to describe or conceive'. Meanwhile the Emperor of Lilliput and his court stand on the shore to await the outcome of 'this great Adventure'. At first they see only the enemy fleet advancing towards them in a 'large Half-Moon' like the Spanish Armada, Gulliver himself being then almost submerged. They conclude that all is lost, but, as the ships draw nearer, Gulliver emerges Gargantua-like from the waves. He hails '*the most puissant Emperor of Lilliput*' and is created a Nardac on the spot (I. v. 38–9).

Gulliver, like a great and successful general, now enters upon his period of greatest celebrity and danger in Lilliput. With characteristic Lilliputian speed and decisiveness the Emperor requests Gulliver to reduce 'the whole Empire of *Blefuscu* into a Province', that it might be governed by a Viceroy; that the Big-Endian exiles might be destroyed, that everyone be compelled to break their eggs at the smaller end, so that the Emperor might be 'sole Monarch of the whole World'. This ambition strikes us as so inordinate that it is easy

to underestimate the importance of the first occasion in Lilliput
when Gulliver refuses to comply with what he is asked to do.
First, 'I endeavoured to divert him from this Design', then:

I plainly protested, that I would never be an Instrument of bringing
a free and brave People into Slavery: And when the Matter was
debated in Council, the wisest Part of the Ministry were of my Opinion.
(I. v. 39–40)

The Emperor is displeased. Gulliver is now on the slippery
slope. He next offends by talking with the Blefuscudian ambassadors in Mildendo to sue for peace, and actually requests
the Emperor of Lilliput's permission to visit the Emperor of
Blefuscu. This is a false step. Permission is given very coldly.
Then comes something unexpected. An outbreak of fire in the
Empress's part of the palace is too much for the Lilliputian
firefighters. They call for Gulliver who, without the means of
beating out the flames, has no other recourse but the one
which would have occurred to Rabelais. Having fortunately
drunk a lot of wine that evening, and still more fortunately
happened not yet to have discharged any part of it, Gulliver,
with careful aim, effectively extinguishes the fire. To save the
Empress and the palace he has committed a capital offence:
worse, he has violated a taboo of Lilliputian society.

At this point something strange happens in the style of
the book. A temporary transformation occurs in Gulliver's
narrative. The satirical account of an all too recognizable
political world is checked, and, with chapter 6, Gulliver starts
to describe the legal, social and educational practice of Lilliput
as if he were Hythloday recommending the customs of Utopia.
He briefly outlines the admirable measures they take against
informers, false witnesses, and those guilty of fraud and breach
of trust. They reward the law-abiding, and have regard to
morality when they promote to positions of trust. (The antics
of Flimnap seem quite forgotten.) 'Disbelief of a Divine Providence' precludes a man from public office, and 'Ingratitude'
is a 'capital Crime' (I. vi. 47). There is a rigorously rational
system of bringing up children based on a disapproval of
emotion and affection. Children are prepared for a profession

appropriate to the rank of their parents. Girls are trained almost as severely as boys (but with frightful penalties for their female mentors if they lapse below male standard of education). Young Ladies are to be as brave and wise as men, though the prospect of a domestic life allows their physical exercises to be 'not altogether so robust' and their 'Compass of Learning' smaller (I. vi. 48–9).

This change – to the idiom of one disclosing an ideal society – can be explained on two levels. Swift does not wish to become locked into a single literary mode: he wishes if possible to disturb and provoke. But this does not license arbitrary interpolation, and the placing of the passage within the larger text is most adroit. Given colour by Gulliver's announced intention to write in the future a full account of Lilliputian society, of which the earlier part of chapter 6 is but a sketch, his account reveals a grave disjunction between profession and practice. The reader has not seen a society of this kind in action. On the contrary, he has seen Flimnap capering on a tightrope to stay in Office, and will shortly see the person to whom Lilliput has most cause for gratitude in danger of impeachment. Either Lilliput is not at one with itself, preaching what it does not practise, or Gulliver has deceived himself. In either case he is unable to put together his conventional Utopian account of Lilliputian society and his plain narrative of what happens to him in Lilliput, and come to a comprehensive conclusion.

As the narrative resumes, Lilliput is revealed as totally treacherous and ungrateful. Flimnap, the Lord Treasurer, looks on Gulliver with a sour face, and privately complains of the cost of feeding him. Bolgolam, the Admiral, is jealous of his naval adventure. The Emperor's politeness means nothing. Gulliver is confidentially informed that Articles of Impeachment have been prepared against him, alleging the capital crime of pissing on the palace, disobedience to the Emperor in not destroying Blefuscu, and traitorous links with the ambassadors and court of the enemy nation. There is a debate about whether Gulliver should be killed, and how, with Flimnap and Golgolam recommending the severest penalty, and the Emperor urging, or seeming to urge, his many services to the state. The matter is compromised after many concili- atory interventions by Gulliver's friend Secretary Reldresal: Gulliver will not be killed outright, but only have his eyes put out, and thereafter be gradually starved to death. This decision is as intelligent as we have come to expect from Lilliput. The Emperor shows his 'great *Lenity*' (a word much insisted on here, signalling a quotation from Suetonius on the tyrant Domitian) by not having Gulliver publicly executed. Even blinded, Gulliver will still be able, like Samson, to serve the state for a certain time. And then the method of killing Gulliver will save the great cost of feeding him. As Gulliver retrospectively tells of the decision he now takes to make his escape from Lilliput, he fears censure, and is rather on the defensive. As he points out, in one of Swift's finest ironies, 'if I had then known the Nature of Princes and Ministers, which I have since observed in many other Courts, and their Methods of treating Criminals less obnoxious than myself; I should with great Alacrity and Readiness have submitted to so *easy* a Punish- ment'. (The words 'Alacrity' and 'Readiness' are especially comic and mordant.) As it is, however, 'hurried on by the Precipitancy of Youth' (I. vii. 61), he flees to Blefuscu where he is well received, discovers and repairs a real boat in which he 'ventures himself in the Ocean' and is eventually picked up by an English ship. He is thus enabled to return to his 'beloved Country, and the dear Pledges I had left in it': his family (I. viii. 67). A businesslike paragraph of financial and family detail restores Gulliver to the real world.

As Part I reaches its conclusion we have to ask some ques- tions about Gulliver and the Emperor of Lilliput. Who or what is Gulliver, and what is his part in Swift's text? Such has been Swift's attention to realizing the physical world of Lilliput that it has hardly occurred to the reader to take Gulliver for anything other than a responsible, more or less represen- tative Englishman. His chief feature, indeed, is his gentleness and co-operativeness towards the Lilliputians, which a typical Englishman might not have shown to a race of midgets who took him prisoner. In effect Gulliver shows civility, and a readiness to learn and serve. His *volte face* in refusing to destroy Blefuscu (the first time he refuses to be an instrument of the Emperor) seems in the circumstances natural, and if we think this, if we are even a little relieved to find a limit to Gulliver's co-operation, we have come to think of him as a character. This is a significant conclusion, since the author of *A Tale of a Tub* has previously filled his texts with figures who are chiefly names, or types, or masks, or mouthpieces, but do not begin to be characters in the way that, for example, Defoe's Crusoe is a character. Even when seen in a single voyage only, Gulliver takes on something of this kind of life, though we must remember that characters can also be used as spokesmen for the author, examples for approval or ridicule, allusions to historical figures, and so forth.

This brings us to the Emperor. If Reldresal's account of war and party in Lilliput alludes to early eighteenth-century England, can the Emperor allude to some historical figure? He expresses the views of the War Party, the more extreme Whigs, and recalls William III who originally took England into the war (they share a hooked nose) and George I who had wished the war to continue (his '*Austrian* Lip' suggests the anti-French coalition). Like George I the Emperor relies on one party only, and that the less numerous, to form his governments. The Emperor is thus a composite figure, representing no one historical individual: the insatiable warlike prince, he expresses a particular tendency within recent English history. In the same way Gulliver, who gave the Emperor his victory but refused to subjugate the foe, suggests in this context those in the government Swift had supported who, having prosecuted the war, negotiated the peace, and were subsequently in danger of death for so doing. Ormonde, who had replaced Marlborough as Commander in Chief, and St John who achieved the Treaty of Utrecht, both fled to France under threat of impeachment early in the new reign. If then the reader at this juncture is inclined to approve of Gulliver as a character, he also endorses a certain political stand: that of the Tory government in the four last years of the Queen.

The tradition of political interpretation of *Gulliver's Travels* has not hesitated to identify figures in the text with historical individuals. The line goes back from Ehrenpreis through Case and Firth to the first readers of Swift's book. Thinly veiled histories, together with keys and clues to interpret them, were certainly published during Swift's lifetime, and this expectation in reading helped to create an interest in works which did not always aim at satisfying it. Writing a book obviously indebted to Rabelais, Swift probably remembered Peter Motteux's particular interpretations of *Gargantua and Pantagruel*, Bks IV and V. Almost certainly Swift played on his readership's expectation of finding originals in his text. If, however, political allegory, for want of a better term, depends on a consistent one-to-one relation between textual figure and historical figure, *Gulliver's Travels* is not a political allegory, as F. P. Lock has recently shown. But the great error in all this (from which Lock is not entirely free) is to assume that if no one-to-one political relations can be demonstrated, the work in question can make no particular political allusion at all, but must work on the level of the blandest generalities concerning the ambition of princes, the perils of success, and so forth. 'Discontinuous political allegory' – a notion that has been found useful in recent years for an understanding of both Dryden's *The Hind and the Panther* and Mann's *Dr Faustus* – is a term more likely to help us see what Swift is doing. Swift maintains the life of the general and the particular by keeping them simultaneously in mind. He keeps up our sense of the possibility of identification, offering, sometimes, almost enough to establish it. Thus it is, perhaps, with one of the very earliest 'identifications' proposed: that of Flimnap, the Emperor's Lord High Treasurer, with Robert Walpole, Treasurer and 'prime minister' in George I's administrations after 1721 (I. iii. 25; vi. 52; Turner, p. 319). We might expect the most powerful politician of his day to have some life in Swift's text.

Chapter 5

A voyage to Brobdingnag

If Lilliput hardly proved a '*South-Sea*' to Lemuel Gulliver, his return to England saw his family out of their financial straits and comfortably established 'in a good House at Redriff'. A modest inheritance within his family brought this improvement about. His promising son Johnny was now at Grammar School and doing well; his daughter Betty was learning needlework (I. viii. 69). Curiosity to see new foreign lands, rather than financial gain, induced Gulliver to make a further voyage, and embark on the *Adventure*, bound for Surat, under the command of Captain John Nicholas of Liverpool. 'Nature and Fortune', he explicitly says, 'condemned' him to an active and restless life (II. i. 73).

The reader embarks upon the Voyage to Brobdingnag with certain expectations. First, we expect a clear, practical, physical narrative which will familiarize, if not demystify, the marvellous. Secondly, we are now well-disposed to Gulliver. On the basis of Part I we expect in him a character well-disposed and civil towards any strange peoples he may encounter, but not merely a passive follower of their ways. We think Gulliver has a mind of his own, and a capacity for moral independence and individual action.

These expectations are, and are not, fulfilled. Having adjusted to the diction of Part I the reader is jolted somewhat to encounter, early in Part II, a passage of sheer tarpaulin:

Finding it was like to overblow, we took in our Sprit-sail, and stood by to hand the Fore-sail; but making foul Weather, we looked the Guns were all fast, and handed the Missen. The Ship lay very broad off, so we thought it better spooning before the Sea than trying or hulling. We reeft the Foresail and set him, we hawled aft the Foresheet; the Helm was hard a Weather. The Ship wore bravely. We belay'd the Foredown-hall; but the Sail was split, and we hawl'd

down the Yard, and got the Sail into the Ship, and unbound all the
things clear of it. It was a very fierce Storm; the Sea broke strange and
dangerous. We hawl'd off upon the Lanniard of the Wipstaff ...

(II. i. 74)

and so on for as much again. Dampier acknowledged that he
had 'divested' himself of 'Sea-Phrases' to gratify the 'Land
Reader; for which the Seamen will hardly forgive me' (Preface
to *A New Voyage*). Swift, perhaps, takes this opportunity
of displaying Gulliver's professional familiarity with 'Sea-
Phrases', but the sudden plunge into nautical language (for
which Swift had plundered a passage in Samuel Sturmy's
Mariner's Magazine 1669) is irresistibly comic and, like the
Utopian discourse in 'A Voyage to Lilliput', is a sign of Swift's
unashamed readiness to change his mode when the right opportunity occurs. His narrative has thus a variable relation with
the world.

Almost at once Gulliver reverts to his usual narrative clarity
and plain style for a transition into the marvellous. What
follows is a triumph of the commonplace and almost casual
manner. Having landed on a barren and rocky coast to look
for water and finding none, Gulliver returns to the shore only
to see 'our Men already got into the Boat, and rowing for
Life to the Ship. I was going to hollow after them, although
it had been to little purpose, when I observ'd a huge Creature
walking after them in the Sea, as fast as he could ...' Running
inland in terror, he sees from high ground a meadow with
grass twenty feet tall. He comes to a field of corn 'rising at
least forty Foot' and 'Trees so lofty that I could make no
Computation of their Altitude' (II. i. 75). The monsters who
now come to reap the harvest are as tall as church-spires and
with voices like thunder high in the air. In a desperate attempt to
hide from them and escape, Gulliver squeezes himself between
the corn stalks until he comes to a part where the corn has
been laid by rain and wind. Here he cannot get through, the
fallen ears pierce his clothes and hurt him, and as the giant
reapers draw near he lies down wholly 'overcome by Grief and
Despair' (II. i. 76). As he waits to be discovered, like a small
wild creature from the last corner of the harvest field, he is

able to reflect on how he had appeared to the Lilliputians as these monsters now appeared to him. It is a most interesting moment, establishing Gulliver's mental continuity between the two different worlds of the first two Parts. An educated man, he recalls those philosophers (most recently Swift's countryman Berkeley) who have taught that 'nothing is great or little otherwise than by Comparison', but neither this, nor his own recollections of Lilliput can eradicate from his mind the totally inconsistent opinion that the larger creatures are the 'more Savage and cruel in Proportion to their Bulk ...' Nothing can be more natural than that Gulliver, in his present crisis, should expect 'to be a Morsel in the Mouth of the first among these enormous Barbarians who should happen to seize' him, yet *he* had not behaved barbarously to Lilliput or Blefuscu, while Lilliput had planned to behave barbarously to him. Gulliver is unable to put his two experiences together so as to come to an adequate comparative judgement. Meanwhile one of the giant reapers looks as if he will tread on Gulliver by accident, Gulliver screams, and the reaper spots him, pausing to consider 'with the Caution of one who endeavours to lay hold on a small dangerous Animal in such a Manner that it shall not be able either to scratch or bite him; as I my self have sometimes done with a *Weasel* in *England*' (II. i. 77). Swift has managed Gulliver's transition into a new world of wonders with extraordinary physical and psychological imagination.

Whatever he expects, Gulliver is not devoured by the giant reaper. He is treated gently enough. But he becomes the possession of the local farmer, and is shown for money around the country inns as a midget monster. Eventually he is taken to the capital, Lorbulgrud, where he comes to the attention of the royal court. His health breaking down 'by the continual Drudgery of entertaining the Rabble every Hour of the Day', Gulliver manages to attract the sympathy of the Queen. In response to her question whether he would like to come and live at Court Gulliver, in a moment comparable to that between Crusoe and Friday, says he is his master's 'Slave' but, if free, would be proud to devote his life to her 'Service'. The Queen then purchases him, and Glumdalclitch, the farmer's nine-year old daughter, who was the first Brobdingnagian to be kind to him and look after him, is allowed to stay with him at Court.

'A Voyage to Brobdingnag' is not only different from 'A Voyage to Lilliput' in its reversal of the physical relation of Gulliver with his host people, though that is its simplest and most striking effect. In Part I Gulliver uses a giant's strength with care, judgement and success. In the grip of a military crisis, Lilliput affords him the opportunity to act and a dramatic relation develops between the two, in which Gulliver becomes first the hero, then the alleged traitor, of Lilliput. Brobdingnag, by contrast, is a stable country. There is no external enemy, while internal dissensions between monarch, nobles and people have been happily compromised by the grandfather of the present King (II. vii. 133). In Brobdingnag Gulliver's capacity as a man of action is limited either to mere performance for the interest of spectators, or self-defence in ridiculous and humiliating situations. The reader, whose sympathies with Gulliver have been endorsed by the outcome of the previous Part, shares a measure of his frustration at a predicament in which energy and action can achieve nothing. Part II proceeds in two main ways. First it focuses on the inevitable humiliations of Gulliver and on his midget's eye view of the physical life of the giants. Secondly but more importantly it concentrates on something that never happened in Lilliput: the long series of conversations between Gulliver and the King concerning society and government. Here we come to see that if the physical action of Part II is little more than a series of frustrations, it constitutes a psychological action of considerable interest. It will be right to give brief consideration to each of these aspects of the book.

Gulliver's first show of bravery (it may be thought) was when he outfaced the farmer's wife's fierce-looking, purring, cat (three times larger than an ox): the cat drew back. Soon after, he is assailed at night by two rats and kills one with his sword, wounding the other. This is comparable to slaying certain dragons. On another occasion 'a small white' Brobdingnagian 'Spaniel' (a well-trained dog) follows his scent, picks him up in its mouth, and brings him faithfully to its master. Much less pleasant is the pet monkey belonging to one of the Clerks of the Kitchen which carries Gulliver off, though Glumdalclitch eventually rescues him. A stream of such incidents, including much trouble with small birds and flies, stretches through most of Part II. Swift gives them great emphasis. Some of these episodes are recounted with special humour. Gulliver himself, who shows occasional signs of reverting to the mentality of a small boy, ruefully recounts how, finding a 'Cow-dung' in his path, 'I must needs try my Activity by attempting to leap over it.' Of course he jumps short and returns home 'filthily bemired' (II. v. 117). This is another moral episode in miniature, like Flimnap's capering on the tightrope, but the humour lies in the embarrassed tone of Gulliver's subsequent narrative ('I must needs try my Activity ...'). After Gulliver sails his boat in the artificial pond made for him, to the delight of the Queen and her ladies, Glumdalclitch always carries the boat into her closet and hangs it 'on a Nail to dry' (II. v. 113). The Court dwarf ('I verily think he was not full Thirty Foot high') is a particular trial to Gulliver, always affecting to swagger and look big when he passes him, and seldom failing 'of a smart Word or two upon my Littleness; against which I could only revenge myself by calling him *Brother*, challenging him to wrestle; and such Repartees as are usual in the Mouths of *Court Pages*' (II. iii. 99). This humour is perhaps the very foundation of *Gulliver's Travels* though it is generally more understated, often developed satirically, and sometimes tragically.

More disconcerting than Gulliver's many humiliations, which the kindly Glumdalclitch retails to the laughing royal family and court, is Gulliver's vision of the bodily life of the giants. This is not just a matter of size but of what the microscopic eye can see. In another significant recollection of Lilliput, Gulliver recalls a friend of his there finding a close view of his face 'a very shocking Sight': 'great Holes' apparent in his skin, bristles stronger than those of a boar, and unpleasant differences of colour. This is now how Gulliver sees the Brobdingnagians. The Lilliputians had seemed to Gulliver 'the fairest in the World' (II. i. 82) but now a horror of fleshly life is revealed to him: 'the Woman with a Cancer in her Breast, swelled to a

monstrous Size, full of Holes ... a Fellow with a Wen in his
Neck, larger than five Woolpacks ... But, the most hateful
Sight of all was the Lice crawling on their Cloaths: I could see
distinctly the Limbs of these Vermin ...' (II. iv. 105). Unfor-
tunately the horror is not confined to the diseased and poor.
The Queen is a moderate and fastidious eater, but the sight of
her at dinner is to Gulliver terrifying. The maids of honour are
young, healthy and beautiful. Since they hardly see in Gulliver
a serious sexual partner, they do not hesitate to strip and dress
in his presence: their skin appears coarse, with 'Hairs hanging
from it thicker than Pack-threads.' Swift here becomes outrageously surreal in combining the sexually titillating with the
disconcerting: Gulliver does not appreciate being set, by the
best-looking and most 'frolicksome' maid of honour, 'astride
upon one of her Nipples ...' (II. v. 111–12). The reader is
likely to be divided in response to this moment. The wider
implications, in which Swift is seen to be a Rabelais with a
remarkably different feeling about the physical, show him
writing as an heir of the French philosopher Descartes and the
English poet Rochester, both well known to Swift. In each
case the sheer rigour of their sceptical analysis led them to
the *impasse* which a twentieth-century philosopher, Gilbert
Ryle, has memorably designated the error of 'the Ghost in the
Machine': the spirit in the body. They could not see, as some
earlier thinkers and poets could, the spiritual *expressed* by
bodily life, bodily life lending vigour to the life of the spirit.
Gulliver's un-Rabelaisian, microscopic eye in Brobdingnag, his
fastidious and world-weary eye in the land of the Houyhnhnms,
is the eye that has envisioned one of the most terrifying things
the world can display to human view: living but unanimated
matter, the 'Wen ... larger than five Woolpacks', mindless
growth.

   This mind-and-body dilemma is underlined when we turn
to the second aspect of Part II, the conversations between
Gulliver and the King of Brobdingnag. Unlike the Emperor
of Lilliput the King is interested to hear what Gulliver can
tell him about Europe. Gulliver himself introduces the first
conversation in a thoroughly candid way, paying tribute to the

King's clear apprehension, exact judgements and wise observations, while at the same time admitting that he himself had
been 'a little too copious in talking of my own beloved Country',
its trade, wars, schisms, parties and prejudices. Gulliver here
plays something of the part of Reldresal in Lilliput, though
unlike the Lilliputian he does not have an urgent political
motive for his discourse. By the same token Gulliver's serious
practical response to Reldresal is contrasted with that of the
giant king to Gulliver:

> he could nor forbear taking me up in his right Hand, and stroaking
> me gently with the other; after an hearty Fit of laughing, asked me
> whether I were a *Whig* or a *Tory*. Then turning to his first Minister,
> who waited behind him with a white Staff, near as tall as the Main-
> mast of the Royal *Sovereign*, he observed, how contemptible a Thing
> was human Grandeur, which could be mimicked by such diminutive
> Insects as I ... And thus he continued on, while my Colour came
> and went several Times, with Indignation to hear our noble Country,
> the Mistress of Arts and Arms, the Scourge of France, the Arbitress
> of Europe, the Seat of Virtue, Piety, Honour and Truth, the Pride
> and Envy of the World, so contemptuously treated.   (II. iii. 98–9)

This passage is wonderfully structured around the idea of
relative scale, and the corresponding political implications.
Gulliver, in the palm of the King's hand, suddenly discloses
(in his subsequent narrative) the physical height of the Minister's
symbol of authority ('as tall as the Main-mast of the Royal
Sovereign'): the issue of Whig or Tory (to which Swift had
committed much of his life) is then made the object of hearty
laughter and Gulliver is called a diminutive insect. The reader's
vision has been made to focus down, enlarge and focus down
again, before Gulliver, turning red and pale by turns with
mortification, vainly attempts to enlarge the minds of his hearers
with the alleged greatness of his native land. It will be noticed
that what the King finds contemptible is something in his own
world: human grandeur. His line of thought is to find something
in the discourse of a stranger that he can apply to his own
situation, though it is not of course what Gulliver hopes he will
learn. Somehow Gulliver cannot avoid getting laughed at.
Worse is to come. Wearied with entertaining the Court and

being an object of ridicule, he remarks to the King one day 'That, Reason did not extend itself with the Bulk of the Body', that among other animals bees and ants had the reputation of being more wise and industrious than many larger creatures, and that even he, Gulliver, might give the King information which would be valuable to him. Gulliver's mention of bees and ants reminds us of the bee in *The Battle of the Books*, whose discoveries of pollen are digested and transformed into the honey and wax of wisdom. True to this humanist ideal, the giant king listens attentively while Gulliver wishing for the Tongue of Demosthenes or Cicero, launches into 'the Praise of my own dear native Country'.

We have already seen Gulliver in the rather misleading rôle of Utopian narrator, in chapter 6 of Part I. Swift now rings a further change on this idea. Gulliver does not consider his discourses properly Utopian; from his viewpoint he is offering a well-deserved panegyrical history of Great Britain. From the King's point of view, on the other hand, inclined as he is to think that Britain may exist, listening to Gulliver is like Morus listening to Hythloday in *Utopia*. Gulliver covers every aspect of the political and social structure of this allegedly ideal commonwealth; it takes five interviews to get through it all, and the King makes a lot of notes. Then, in a sixth interview, the King asks questions and makes his own observations. These remarks are admirably telling and practical, and are a form of satire in themselves. On the topic of new promotions to the nobility the King asked: 'Whether the Humour of the Prince, a Sum of Money to a Court-Lady, or a Prime Minister; or a Design of strengthening a Party opposite to the Publick Interest, ever happened to be Motives in those Advancements' (II. vi. 122)? The humour and irony lie in the words 'ever happened'. Again, the King asked about how and why people in Britain sought to become members of the House of Commons: 'How it came to pass, that People were so violently bent upon getting into this Assembly, which I allowed to be a great Trouble and Expense, often to the Ruin of their Families, without any Salary or Pension: Because this appeared such an exalted Strain of Virtue and publick Spirit, that his Majesty seemed to doubt it might possibly not be always sincere' (II. vi. 123). Here the humour lies not only in the tentativeness of the concluding question (set against the obviousness of the evidence), but in our uncertainty as to whether the King or Gulliver is responsible for the delicacy of formulation. On the legal system of Britain the King, in a more decisive question, asked: 'Whether Party in Religion or Politicks were observed to be of any Weight in the Scale of Justice' (II. vi. 124). As to the recent history of Gulliver's native land, 'he was amazed to hear me talk of a mercenary standing Army in the midst of Peace, and among a free People' and, of 'our Affairs during the last Century' protested that the history was only 'an Heap of Conspiracies, rebellions, Murders, Massacres, Revolutions, Banishments ...' (II. vi. 124–5). In a seventh and final interview the King sums up his conclusions. He is willing to accept that Gulliver himself, a traveller, may have escaped many of the vices of his country but, he says, in the most quoted passage from the whole of the *Travels*, 'I cannot but conclude the Bulk of your Natives, to be the most pernicious Race of little odious Vermin that Nature ever suffered to crawl upon the Surface of the Earth' (II. vi. 126).

At this Gulliver is filled with resentment. He admits to artfully eluding the thrust of the King's questions so far as possible, and to presenting his native land in the most favourable possible light. We perceive that the King's devastating criticisms are a blend of obvious generalization on self-interest in public life and of specific Tory positions on matters such as standing armies and war, taxes and the national debt. Gulliver, by contrast, now emerges as a devious patriot and a ranting Whig, resolved to dismiss the King's substantial objections to the condition of Britain as the '*Narrowness* of *Thinking*' inevitable in a King 'wholly secluded from the rest of the World ...' (II. vii. 127). Gulliver's idea is now not to argue back, certainly not to admit he is in the wrong, but to 'ingratiate' himself further in the King's favour by offering him something powerful. He seeks to compel the King's respect by giving him the secret of gunpowder, describing with some relish the effect of this invention, and how useful it might be to the monarch if his metropolis should ever 'pretend to dispute his absolute Commands'. The King is 'struck with Horror at the Description I had given of these terrible Engines ... A strange Effect of *narrow* Principles and *short Views*!' (II. vii. 129).

Swift's larger strategy in Parts I and II now comes clearly into view. He has been working all the time with the reader's viewpoint in mind. In Part I Gulliver (save a little solemn naivety) won the approval of the reader by his conduct and judgement. His goodwill, and moderation, and the real danger he is in at the end, win as much sympathy from the reader as the hero of such an impossible tale could possibly gain. At the beginning of Part II, therefore, the reader is inclined to identify with Gulliver and, despite implications to the contrary, to share his evident fear that if the diminutive Lilliputians ended by treating him badly, the monstrous Brobdingnagians are bound to treat him worse. This barbarous treatment does not come about. Once at court he is kindly treated though an object of repeated ridicule. The reader continues to identify with Gulliver, laughing at him indeed, but uncomfortably aware of how we should feel in his shoes, until the time of Gulliver's political conversations with the King. Then our sympathy with him is in a few pages completely shattered: indeed, the King's condemnation is felt the more strongly because the reader has been so close to Gulliver. Swift's shaping of the fable of Parts I and II has deprived the reader of any position of detachment from which the King's judgement could be assessed. The satirical rhetoric of Swift's first two voyages has turned entirely on this issue of identification with and alienation from Gulliver. We realize that we are 'the most pernicious Race of little odious Vermin that Nature ever suffered to crawl upon the Surface of the Earth' and that it is Gulliver's implausible and excessive patriotism, glorification of war and admiration of power, that has brought this judgement down on us.

The symmetries of Swift's first two voyages are not therefore merely physical: Gulliver the giant among midgets, Gulliver the midget among giants. We see that the physical situation affects the moral outlook. It is easier for Gulliver to be moderate and benevolent in Lilliput, despite the vicious ingenuity of the Lilliputians, than to be so in Brobdingnag, where his very size means that he is perpetually laughed at and humiliated. Thus the steady Tory of Part I becomes the war-crazed Whig of Part II. It is also notable that the Emperor of Lilliput only wants to use Gulliver as the ultimate weapon in his war. The King of Brobdingnag, on the other hand, pays attention to all that Gulliver tells him. He really hopes to learn something, especially on fiscal policy. The Emperor of Lilliput is the Tory view of a Whig king. The King of Brobdingnag is the Tory view of a Tory king, that is to say he governs a stable and peaceful commonwealth, without party, and his judgements only take on a contentious edge when controverting some Whig innovation of which Gulliver informs him. The King is the father of his people, but his kingdom is still (though gigantic) part of the real world: there is disease, poverty, greed and vanity. Finally the two books contrast with and complement each other in regard to the relation between Gulliver and the reader, the trust which has grown up through Part I being broken by the end of Part II.

Still, Gulliver longs to regain what it is natural for him to think of as his 'Liberty' and to return to his family ('those domestick Pledges') in his native land. This wish is accomplished, not through any effort on Gulliver's part, but in a wonderful and Cyrano-like way. One day at the seaside a giant eagle carries away Gulliver's travelling box with Gulliver inside. In due course it is dropped into the sea, from which he is fortunate enough to be rescued by an English ship which brings him home. The captain will take no payment for his passage and even lends Gulliver five shillings. Gulliver has no religious thoughts on what many would have considered a providential deliverance, but comments darkly on the 'evil Destiny' which would take him again to sea. Meanwhile he feels like a giant and everyone else seems to him like a pigmy.

Chapter 6

A voyage to Laputa, Balnibarbi, Luggnag, Glubbdubdrib, and Japan

Nothing is more striking in the composition of *Gulliver's Travels* than that Swift wanted to place Part III where he did, for it was evidently written *after* Part IV, and then deliberately inserted in its present position (Ehrenpreis, III.443–4). It is traditional, even automatic, to compare Part III unfavourably with the other parts of the *Travels*, but Swift's intentions in proceeding from 'A Voyage to the Houhnhnms' to the composition of a further Voyage, and then so decisively altering the order of composition seem to have been very little considered. In the absence of explicit authorial statement the best way of doing this is to carry out an open-minded critical exploration of Part III in relation to the *Travels* as a whole. And, to wipe the slate clean, it should be said here that there is no direct evidence that Part III uses earlier satiric materials discussed by Swift with his friends Arbuthnot, Gay and Pope, in the last years of Queen Anne (Ehrenpreis, III.445). Arbuthnot's own feeling that, had he known of Swift's design, he 'could have added such abundance of things upon every subject' is evidence against this claim. Another often repeated claim, that Swift's satiric friends were less satisfied with Part III than the rest of the *Travels* comes down to Gay's report that 'Critics ... think the flying island is the least entertaining' and Swift's statement to Pope that 'Dr Arbuthnot likes the Projectors least, others you tell me the Flying Island ...' (*Heritage*, pp. 63–4). These comments are comparative, concern only parts of Part III, and were made in the context of high appreciation of the newly published book.

Gulliver had not been home from Brobdingnag ten days when Captain William Robinson, an old acquaintance, came to his house and persuaded him to be Surgeon in his ship the Hope-well on a new voyage to the *East-Indies*. This new transition to a world of wonders, by now a convention within the text of the *Travels*, is more elaborate than usual. Gulliver is easily persuaded by compliments, promises of higher status, and the offer of double pay, to go on the new voyage, but this time Mrs Gulliver has to be persuaded too, and only agrees because of 'the Prospect of Advantage' to her children (III. i. 150). The ship sets sail on 5 August 1706 and, after touching in Madras ('Fort St George') they press on to Tonking. Here Gulliver becomes Master of a sloop purchased by Captain Robinson and sets sail in her while Robinson himself remains behind to trade. Battered by a great storm, Gulliver is immediately after attacked by a crew of Japanese pirates, who include a Dutchman. This Dutchman is far more ferocious than the Japanese. When Gulliver (a war-Whig, we remember, in Part II) reminds him that they were both Christians and Protestants from neighbouring countries in strict alliance, the year being 1707 and the War of the Spanish Succession in full spate, the Dutchman's rage is the more inflamed. The pagan Japanese treat Gulliver better than the Dutchman proposes, and grant him his life, but the outcome is that he is set adrift in a canoe with only four days' rations. Gulliver's fellow men seem to treat him worse as his voyages go on. In this way Gulliver finds several islands, on the last of which there are rocks, grass, herbs, birds' eggs, and Gulliver's account of this shore is perhaps the fullest in the *Travels*. 'I gathered Plenty of Eggs upon the Rocks, and got a Quantity of dry Seaweed, and parched Grass, which I designed to kindle the next Day, and roast my Eggs as well as I could ...' Despite these natural advantages Gulliver is almost in despair when he considers 'how impossible it was to preserve my Life in so desolate a Place; and how miserable my End must be' (III. i. 152). Oppressed in broad day by the fierce heat of the sun, Gulliver is unexpectedly aware of relief from the shadow of 'a vast Opake Body': it proves to be the flying Island of Laputa. Once again, as Gulliver sees 'this vast Body' descending, with numbers of people moving up and down the sides of it, one might expect him to give thanks to God for what promised to be a miraculous delivery 'from the desolate Place and Condition

I was in' but all he feels is some 'inward Motion of Joy' from 'the natural Love of Life' (p. 153). Soon he is taken up into the flying island.

From one point of view the Court of Laputa is an example of high civilization. The King and his courtiers are entirely preoccupied with abstract and intellectual pursuits. All their concern is with mathematics, astronomy and music. One of their eyes is turned ever inward, but the other 'directly up to the Zenith'. So intense is their mental speculation that they need servants with flappers to recall them gently to their immediate circumstances. Gulliver is received into the royal presence to find the King surrounded by 'Persons of prime Quality' and seated before a table filled with 'Globes and Spheres, and Mathematical Instruments of all Kinds'. He takes no notice of Gulliver for an hour, until he has solved a problem on which he is then working (III. ii. 155–6). The King of Laputa, is a richly absurd amalgam of some of the tendencies Swift had attacked in his earlier work. The Laputans partly remind us of Jack, in *A Tale of a Tub*, who has so much inner light that he is perpetually colliding with external objects. Again, the spider in *A Battle of the Books* was an emblem of the false self-sufficiency (as Swift saw the situation) of that range of intellectual activities which stretched from mathematics and theory to engineering and fortification. Neither is willing to learn from lives and needs outside himself, to travel and digest like the bee. The King and court of Laputa further exemplify this attitude to human life. In the *Travels* this monarch displays a quite new attitude to Gulliver. Unlike the Emperor of Lilliput, he does not attempt to use Gulliver as a weapon; unlike the King of Brobdingnag he does not listen to what he has to say and try to learn from it, or scarcely so. Once Gulliver has learned Laputan, he has a second audience of the King. 'His Majesty discovered not the least Curiosity to enquire into the Laws, Government, History, Religion, or Manners of the Countries where I had been; but confined his Questions to the State of Mathematicks, and received the Account I gave him, with great Contempt and Indifference, though often roused by his *Flapper* on each Side' (III. ii. 163). We can see that the

King of Laputa exemplifies just as significant a human attitude to Gulliver as the two earlier rulers. The consequence of this attitude, however, is that Gulliver himself is afforded no dramatic rôle. He need display neither the courteous and co-operative deference he shows in Lilliput, nor the assertive activity and loquacity he shows in Brobdingnag. He is neither the hero, the traitor, nor the mortified clown of this court. Though he thinks the flying island 'the most delicious Spot of Ground in the World' (III. ii. 162), in Laputa he is generally the unimpressed marginal spectator. This in turn has an important effect on the reader's attitude to him. The distrust and contempt he aroused towards the end of Part II begin to be neutralized. The rehabilitation of Gulliver in the eyes of the reader has begun.

Gulliver, we notice, has been rescued from the fate of Crusoe by science. The flying island is no great object of admiration in the text of the *Travels*, but it demonstrates that the mathematical ethos of the Laputans could achieve something remarkable. Swift's foray into Renaissance science fiction focuses for a time on the 'Loadstone of prodigious Size', fixed on an 'Axle of Adamant', by means of which the island is able to rise or fall, and move from one place to another. This brings us to the recognition that the island 'cannot move beyond the Extent of the Dominions below' (III. iii. 166) which appears at first a purely magnetic point. Gulliver's account is, however, modulating rapidly from the scientific into the political. A government relies for its power, and sometimes even its separateness, on the land it rules. The flying island cannot remain operational beyond the limits of the underlying land. Further, if any town on the land below should refuse tribute or otherwise rebel, it can usually be brought to submission by the island's hovering low down over it to deprive it of sun and rain, or perhaps to enable it to be bombed with rocks. The final penalty would be to let the island drop directly on the rebellious town. The danger of this, however, would be that the island itself might be destroyed and never rise again. We now see that we are confronted by a political emblem concerning the interdependence of court and country, government and people, in accordance with which the ultimate punishment inflicted by the government becomes not just destructive but self-destructive.

At this point modern editions of the *Travels* include a passage of five paragraphs not found in either the first edition by Benjamin Motte in 1726, nor the second by George Faulkner from Dublin in 1735. It derives from an entry in the hand of Swift's friend and editorial confidant, Charles Ford, in his interleaved copy of the first edition now in the Victoria and Albert Museum, London. It seems designed to clinch the foregoing political analysis with a telling example, and describes a very severe confrontation 'About three Years before' between the government on Laputa and Lindalino the second city of the King's territories below. The citizens of Lindalino resolved to resist the oppressions of the government to the last extremity, even siting loadstones to pull the flying island down. In this way the government's bluff was called and the King was obliged to negotiate. The passage concludes, however, on a note of revolutionary violence:

I was assured by a great Minister, that if the Island had descended so near the Town, as not to be able to raise it self, the Citizens were determined to fix it for ever, to kill the King and all his Servants, and entirely change the Government.   (III. iii. 171)

Swift's art in the handling of verbs is evident in this single sentence: the positive, perfect tense ('I was assured ...') at the start, followed by the sagging centre of the sequence with its conditionals ('if the Island had descended ... so as not to be able ...') concluding with the three energetic expressions of future intent: 'determined to fix it for ever, to kill the King ... and entirely change ...'

This passage brings the modern reader to the sharp edge of what was and was not publishable in Swift's time. Though Ford was at some points a disaffected and suspected person, there is no reason to think that he was the author. It appears to be a passage which Swift wrote but had second thoughts about publishing, or which Motte and/or Faulkner refused to publish. Just possibly Swift and Ford regarded it as a dangerous *jeu d'esprit*, never seriously meant for publication in the way that Ford's other corrections and additions in this same copy were. Whichever of these hypotheses is favoured, here is a passage effective within the logical structure of Gulliver's account of Laputa, which somebody judged it imprudent to include in the text in 1726 or 1735. What could be the reason? First and most obviously the explosive nature of the final sentence, with its implications for established governments of any kind. Secondly because, in a work which elsewhere alluded to recent affairs of state and current political values, the passage looked as if it referred to a real recent incident (three years back from 1726?). The most obvious recent example of such a political confrontation in British history, in which the government finally backed down, was certainly the *Drapier's Letters* crisis in which Swift himself had been the champion against the government. On these grounds alone the traditional assumption that this passage alludes to that crisis is probably correct. The implication, then, is that Balnibarbi may be Ireland. This is not allegory as a thinly veiling disguise, and it is wrong to assume that only by such means can contemporary allusion be made. Swift wished to keep up his formal anonymity in both works; Ford, who had been with St John in France in 1715 and been arrested on his return, also had reasons for being careful. Some details, therefore, agree with the *Drapier's Letters* crisis (for example Lindalino has been plausibly decoded to mean Dublin: Turner, p. 346, n. 21) but, like many other parts of the *Travels*, the whole episode is handled in such a way as to hint at more detailed and exact correspondences than can be demonstrated. It imparts to Swift's generalizing analysis of the relation between governors and governed a strong sense of recent mystery and danger, which certainly gives the chapter a climax.

Gulliver's narrative now turns from the flying island to the poverty-stricken and mismanaged country of Balnibarbi beneath. Most commonly remembered from this part of the *Travels* is the account of the Academy in the capital city, Lagado, where many crazy-seeming or revolting experiments are conducted, such as breeding a race of naked sheep, or building houses from the roof down (like the bees and the spiders), or recycling excrement to reduce it 'to its original Food' (III. iv–v. 178–82). In an age which discusses artificial intelligence the thinking machine which is explained to Gulliver may not seem so laughably improbable as it once did, and many of these projects seem to have been chosen with an uncanny instinct for the implausibly possible. It should be noted that within the fiction of this part of the *Travels* the mania for projection and experiment comes from an imperfect understanding of the mathematical wisdom of Laputa (III. iv. 176). This seems to suggest, since the flying island really does fly, that Swift is not condemning all experiment in natural philosophy as doomed to hapless failure. What seems to be satirized here is neglect of the most ready and obvious ways of serving human need. The flying island flies, but only further separates ruler and ruled. Balnibarbi once had a thriving agriculture, but now sinks into poverty and misery because of an ill-judged crash-programme of experiment – there are analogies here with twentieth-century attempts to introduce sophisticated technology into hitherto peasant economies. Swift (who might have agreed with the ideals of intermediate technology) is not attacking science *per se*, but a false assessment of human priorities in science's name. And what of Gulliver's reaction to all this? As Part III proceeds, his initially factual account of what he sees steadily evolves into the intimation of what he feels. His comments on Balnibarbi: 'I never knew a Soil so unhappily cultivated, Houses so ill contrived and so ruinous, or a People whose Countenances and Habit expressed so much Misery and Want' (III. iv. 174), followed by his response to the estate of the unfashionable Lord Munodi: '... in three Hours travelling, the Scene was wholly altered; we came into a most beautiful Country; Farmers Houses at small Distances, neatly built, the Fields enclosed, containing Vineyards, Corngrounds and Meadows ..., His Excellency observed my Countenance to clear up; he told me with a Sigh, that there his Estate began ...' (III. iv. 175) make it clear what Gulliver thinks. This is the more notable because Lord Munodi expresses, in Part III, all that the King of Brobdingnag stood for in Part II. The reader may perhaps think that Gulliver has learned something from the contrast between Brobdingnag and Laputa. At any rate he is getting back into the habit of sharing Gulliver's reactions.

As the flying island turned into a political emblem, so the Academy of Lagado has its School of Political Projectors, with various nasty forms of political activity. George Orwell, a significant witness, saw that Swift 'has an extraordinarily clear prevision of the spy-haunted "police State", with its endless heresy hunts and treason trials ... There is something queerly familiar in the atmosphere of these chapters, because, mixed up with much fooling, there is a perception that one of the aims of totalitarianism is not merely to make sure that people think the right thoughts, but actually to make them *less conscious*' ('Politics *vs* Literature' *Collected Essays*, IV. 213–14). We know more now than Orwell did about Sir Robert Walpole's terrifying intelligence service, which had recently shown what it could do by the arrest of Bishop Francis Atterbury for Jacobite conspiracy. Atterbury was certainly a leading conspirator; on the other hand the evidence against him at his 'trial' in the House of Lords was largely fabricated. Gulliver is commenting on this when he speaks of his own experience to the Political Projectors: 'I told him, that in the Kingdom of *Tribnia* [Britain], by the Natives called *Langden* [London], where I had long sojourned, the Bulk of the People consisted wholly of Discoverers, Witnesses, Informers, Accusers, Prosecutors, Evidences, Swearers ...' (III. vi. 191). Gulliver contributes a sneaky trick or two to the projectors, but his heart hardly seems in it, fortunately.

As we look back on Gulliver's rôle in the first six chapters of Part III we notice a further change. The two earlier Parts were built on the obvious contrast, physical and moral, between Gulliver and the two strange monarchies he visited; these Parts had a twofold structure. In Part III, where Gulliver is more simply a spectator, this structure alters: here we have a threefold structure, Laputa, Balnibarbi, and Gulliver himself moving between the two. This new structure not only contributes a good deal to the renewed convergence between Gulliver and the reader noticed above, but has an important preparatory function for Part IV, which Swift had, of course, already written.

Part III is not yet completed, however. Its five final chapters accomplish yet a further change of mode of the kind we have already noticed in the Utopian passage in Part I, chapter 6, and the paragraph of tarpaulin in Part II, chapter 1. The present and by far the most extensive shift of mode takes us back to *Gargantua and Pantagruel*, not to the earlier books, but the last one, which sets forth the voyage of Pantagruel, Panurge, Friar John and others to the Oracle of the Holy Bottle. Adopting the form of that part of Rabelais' work, Swift sends Gulliver to visit a series of different islands, Glubbdubdribb, Luggnagg, and Japan. This new structural development in the *Travels* is peculiarly fitted to Gulliver's current mood. Early in chapter 6 Gulliver speaks of his 'melancholy' and at the end of it of his desire to return home. The more episodic nature of the voyage to these different islands, by the very multiplication of encounters, increases the implication of weariness on Gulliver's part: the atmosphere is quite different from the still extraordinary verve and inventiveness of *Gargantua and Pantagruel*, Bks IV and V. This is Gulliver's *Vanity of Human Wishes*, or his *Candide*.

On the island of Sorcerers and Magicians, Glubbdubdrib, the Governor is able to call up for Gulliver famous figures from the dead. Gulliver speaks to Alexander the Great, who assures him that he was not poisoned but died of a fever from excessive drinking, and to Hannibal who denied that he used vinegar to cross the Alps. He sees a Roman Senate, the members of which seem like heroes or demi-gods by comparison with a modern one. Caesar and Brutus are raised up, in the latter of whom Gulliver 'could easily discover the most consummate Virtue, the greatest Intrepidity, and Firmness of Mind, the truest Love of his Country, and general Benevolence for Mankind in every Lineament of his Countenance' (III. vii. 196). This is the point where the narrator learns of the unique sextumvirate, Marcus Brutus, Lucius Junius Brutus his ancestor, Socrates, Epaminondas, Cato Uticensis, and Sir Thomas More, who were now perpetually together. All these men exemplify an ethic of individual resistance to 'the higher powers' (Romans, xiii. 1), though in different ways. Socrates, Cato and More have a martyr-like quality in their deaths, but Marcus Brutus, whom Gulliver praises to an extraordinary degree, was, after all, an assassin. Such praise, especially when not balanced by opposing recognitions, as for example in Shakespeare's *Julius Caesar*, places Gulliver in a tradition of principled republican thought going back through Machiavelli to the Roman poet Lucan and historian Tacitus. This antimonarchical inclination is further revealed in the story of the naval captain, whose action was crucial in the defeat of Antony and Cleopatra at the Battle of Actium, thus enabling Octavian to become Augustus. This captain even lost his son in the fight. When he applied for promotion, he was first passed over, and then actually punished, through corruption at the court of the very Augustus praised by so many for his judgement and clemency. In the early eighteenth-century debate concerning the qualities and values of an Augustan Age (see Erskine-Hill, *The Augustan Idea*), Gulliver, or at any rate the Gulliver of Part III, emerges as an anti-Augustan, with a tang of the regicide about him.

Such an attitude, in one who hails from largely monarchical Europe, must entail a special concern with remembering the lessons of republican history. Who can see any sort of historical decline without endorsing Orwell's stress on memory, truth and consciousness? When therefore, on the Island of Luggnagg, Gulliver is informed that there exists there a race of immortals, called the Struldbruggs, he is 'struck with inexpressible Delight' (III. x. 208). If man can be guided by experience, what a contribution to human happiness must an immortal be able to make! Yet Gulliver's informant, while expressing a civil appreciation of his views, is not without a touch of reserve. He asks what Gulliver himself would have hoped to achieve had he been born a Struldbrugg. There follows an enthusiastic outpouring from Gulliver comparable in tone, though not in values, to his praise of his native country to the King of Brobdingnag. It is then pointed out that Gulliver's vision of how a Struldbrugg might wonderfully mend the world is 'unreasonable and unjust, because it supposed a Perpetuity of Youth, Health, and Vigour, which no Man could be so foolish to hope, however extravagant he might be in his Wishes' (III. x. 211–12). This is one of the oldest chestnuts in classical mythology (being granted eternal life, forgetting to request eternal youth): Swift, by his placing the incident in the narrative, and his use of the disillusioned and well-meaning Gulliver as auditor of the story, recovers afresh all its disappointment and horror. The predictable details of the awful old age of the Struldbruggs now follow '... at Ninety they lose their Teeth and Hair; they have at that Age no distinction of Taste ... they can never amuse themselves with reading, because their Memory will not serve to carry them from the Beginning of a Sentence to the End ... The Language of this Country being always upon the Flux, the *Struldbruggs* of one Age do not understand those of another; neither are they able to offer Two Hundred Years to hold any Conversation ...' (III. x. 213–14). No recourse can be had to these immortals to cure the short memory and corruptions of mankind.

Luggnagg is no doubt the climax and anti-climax of Swift's Rabelaisian voyage sequence. Rabelais' voyage was to an oracle, and the wisdom of this oracle was to advise drinking. It has not been sufficiently noticed that one of those classical figures who became caught in the eternal life/eternal youth trap was also an oracle: the Cumaean Sibyl. She appears in this connection in Petronius' *Satyricon*, the most Rabelaisian of Latin classics. Swift, who certainly knew Petronius, has contrived that Gulliver too should sail to an oracle. In his transposition of his Rabelaisian model, however, he destines Gulliver not to an oracle of feasting but to an oracle of death. The wisdom Gulliver gains can be summed up in the reply Trimalchio receives in the *Satyricon*. Seeing with his own eyes the Cumaean Sibyl hanging upside down in a jar: 'I asked, "What would you, Sibyl?"/She answered, "I would die."'

The short final chapter of Part III, though primarily to get Gulliver home, involves one exceptional moment. Gulliver, returning to England by way of Japan, and in the guise of a Dutchman (the Dutch having led the development of European trade there), requests not to have to trample on the crucifix as it was the custom of the Dutch in Japan to do. The Emperor of Japan is surprised at this request, and wonders whether Gulliver may not perhaps be 'a CHRISTIAN' rather than a *Hollander*' (III.xi.218). This Christian reference is one of a series of barbed remarks against the Dutch in this part of the narrative, and is not expanded on. It is as if Gulliver has simply declined to violate some anthropological taboo of his own society, which is how the Japanese seem to see it. The reader, having never found in Gulliver at the most likely moments the introspective religious emotion of Crusoe, and not even the sad prayers of Pantagruel and Panurge as their ship battles with a storm (*Gargantua and Pantagruel*, IV, 20), infers that Gulliver is a conventional Christian only: he may have the answer to the Struldbruggs' message of death, but if so he does not know it. Gulliver's request is, at all events, granted, he proceeds to Nangasic (Nagasaki), whence he takes ship for Amsterdam, and then on to England, arriving at his house in Redriff at 'two in the Afternoon' on 10 April 1710 (III.xi.219).

At this point in the *Travels* several larger critical questions must again be raised. First, concerning Part III itself, how far does the conventional judgement that it is inferior to the other Parts carry conviction? While final consideration must be deferred until the end of reading Part IV, it is already clear that Part III involves, as it were, a change of key. Part III has a new structure, and includes more different encounters. Like Parts I and II it is very political, but its Laputa/Balnibarbi contrast may be thought to prompt a more analytic, generalizing political awareness. On the other hand, a long series of contemporary political allusions conveys to the reader the sense of politics as a dangerous current activity. These points describe an evolution in emphasis: they hardly endorse a falling off in quality.

The rôle of Gulliver must be raised again here. What, or who, does Gulliver seem to be by this stage in the *Travels*? At the end of Part I it seemed fair to think him a character in the relatively undeveloped sense of the early eighteenth century. He seemed more than a *persona*, such as the Hack in *A Tale of a Tub*, or the Proposer in *A Modest Proposal*. Such a conclusion, however, might seem open to challenge at the end of Part II, when Swift has accomplished such a striking satiric contrast-within-symmetry that it is easier than before to see Gulliver as a satiric device or cipher. It is important to recognize that these alternatives are not mutually exclusive. No writer of a stage comedy in the later seventeenth century would have admitted that a successful character could not also have subordinate and active part in a satiric design. The problem for the modern reader is to set aside the expectation of complex and continuous characterization of the sort introduced by Richardson, and developed by Austen, the Brontës, George Eliot and their successors. It may be asked, however, whether in so heavily punctuated a fiction, divided into four different voyages, Gulliver has any continuous existence. In answer it is interesting to observe that in the most sharply contrasting pair of voyages, I and II, Swift is at pains to establish, early in II, Gulliver's capacity to compare his present situation with his past. This argues for continuity. Gulliver does not look back in this way in Part III, yet subtler indications intimate continuity here also. If Gulliver admires Lord Munodi, has he not learned something from the King of Brobdingnag? Does not his naive praise of the idea of immortality remind us of his implausible praise of English glory in Part II? It seems the most natural assumption for the reader to make that there is some continuity in Gulliver from Part to Part. Such an assumption underlies the sense of disillusionment and weariness which pervades the closing chapters of Part III. Certainly Part III closes the moral gulf which had opened between Gulliver and the reader towards the end of Part II. He may not win the reader's complete approval – many of Swift's original readers must have found Gulliver's praise of Marcus Brutus unacceptable – but he shows his benevolence and good judgements on many occasions. This will prove important as we approach Part IV.

The perennial charge that Part III is inferior to Parts I and II is not proven, and should be abandoned. Its excellence is of a different kind from the earlier parts, and this difference is, as we shall now see, a deliberate decision regarding the design of the *Travels* as a whole.

Chapter 7

A voyage to the country of the Houyhnhnms

By comparison with Gulliver's earlier periods at home between voyages he now stays with his wife and family a whole five months, at the end of which Mrs Gulliver is again with child. Then, for the first time, Gulliver has the chance of a command: 'an advantageous Offer made me to be Captain of the *Adventure* ... to trade with the *Indians* in the *South-Sea* ...' (IV.i. 223−4). On this occasion we are not told Mrs Gulliver's view, save that her husband refers to her as 'my poor Wife' (IV.i. 223). If we review the circumstances in which in each of the four voyages Gulliver comes to a strange land, we shall see that he is treated worse as his travels go on. In Part I he is shipwrecked, in Part II deserted at a moment of peril, in Part III abandoned in an open boat by Japanese pirates, and now in Part IV he suffers a mutiny by his crew, is imprisoned on his own ship, and finally set ashore (in his best suit) on the first land they discover, as unknown to them as to Gulliver. 'In this desolate Condition' (IV.i. 224) he has, as usual, no recourse to prayer or religious self-examination. His recent refusal to trample on the crucifix appears to have no implications for him now.

In his new land Gulliver, expecting to find savages, enters a terrain of trees, grass, and several fields of oats. He finds a road on which there are tracks of human feet, of cows, and most of all of horses. What he actually sees first are some strange animals ('At last I beheld several Animals in a Field, and one or two of the same Kind sitting in Trees' − IV.i. 225). He gives a detailed physical description of them, their bodies, where hair grew on them and where it did not, their brown or buff-coloured skin, the different colours of their hair, how they often stood upright, sat down or lay down, how the females were smaller, with less hair on their bodies, and with dugs that hung low down between their 'fore Feet' and often touched

61

the ground as they walked. They are terrifically agile, and with their strong claws 'before and behind' can climb trees 'as nimbly as a Squirrel' (IV. i. 225). The reader expected a description of animals and this has certainly been given. Animals are what these creatures are, but the reader may not at once notice how many of their physical features also apply to that specially graced animal, *homo sapiens*. Gulliver, for his part, does not make this connection. Filled with distaste, he pursues his way, hoping to meet an '*Indian*'. Then he is suddenly confronted by one of the repellent animals head-on: 'The ugly Monster', struck with astonishment, approaches Gulliver and lifts up a 'fore Paw, whether out of Curiosity or Mischief, I could not tell'. Fearing to injure any of the cattle belonging to the 'Inhabitants' of the land, Gulliver merely gives this creature 'a good Blow' with the flat of his sword. It roars with pain, calls its fellows, who come crowding round and compel Gulliver to set his back against a tree to defend himself. However, they take their revenge only by leaping up into the tree and shitting on him. At this crisis a horse is seen 'walking softly in the Field', at which all Gulliver's assailants run away (IV. i. 226).

This is a brilliant piece of psychological, point-of-view narration on Swift's part. Almost none of its careful physical detail would have been inconsistent with an account of very different import: one in which Gulliver, cautiously exploring another strange land, encountered a race of naked people, of whom the first to see him held out his hand, either to greet him, or touch him, or perhaps injure him. When Gulliver struck the first blow, these people did not so much fight back, as mob him, howl at him, and insult him. Nothing inhuman about that.

When we read Part IV for the first time few of us, I think, take these repulsive animals for men and women. Guided by Gulliver's own expectations, and by his choice of words ('Animals ... no Tails ... Claws before and behind ... so disagreeable an Animal ... ugly Monster ... fore Paw'), we share Gulliver's own immediate reaction. The consequences will be seen as events unfold, but such approximation of viewpoint could never have occurred had Part IV followed directly on from the end of Part II. What reader would have been guided by Gulliver's reactions then? It is clear that without the insertion of the later-written Part III to neutralize if not rehabilitate the chauvinistic midget of the later chapters of Part II, the reader's experience of the earlier chapters of Part IV would have been entirely different.

Before these implications have been recognized, the reader's attention is captured by the softly walking horse who so un-expectedly causes the disagreeable animals to disperse. He is startled when he sees Gulliver, walks round him several times, and prevents him from pursuing his way, albeit with 'a very mild Aspect, never offering the least Violence' (IV. i. 226–7). The ever-resourceful Gulliver tries to cajole the obstructive horse by 'using the common Style and Whistle of Jockies' (IV. i. 227) but the horse disdainfully puts up a hoof to prevent his hand. Another horse comes up, and the two greet each other by gently striking each other's right hoofs and neighing. The inspection of Gulliver goes on, and to him the neighing of the horses seems almost articulate. They are extremely per-plexed, but to Gulliver 'the Behaviour of these Animals was so orderly and rational, so acute and judicious, that I at last concluded, they must needs be Magicians, who had thus meta-morphosed themselves upon some Design' (IV. i. 228). For a moment Swift's fiction enters the realm of Apuleius' *Meta-morphosis*, or *The Golden Ass*, in which a man is turned by magic into an ass and eventually back into a man. No magical disclosures follow, however, but Gulliver succeeds in pro-nouncing two of the words which the horses seem to whinny to one another: 'Yahoo' and (more difficult) 'Houyhnhnm' (IV. i. 229). He does not know what they mean. Under instructions he accompanies the original dapple-grey horse to his long, low, timber-and-wattle dwelling place. It is here that the meaning of the two words he has learned is brought home to Gulliver and, worse still, that he is made to recognize that the 'abominable Animal' the Yahoo has in fact 'a perfect human Figure' (IV. ii. 232). He acknowledges to himself that he is what the Houyhnhnms call a Yahoo, and that the only reason why they do not yet realize this is that his clothes make his body look different. He has no trouble in rejecting the various samples of Yahoo food offered to him, and is able to display an unfeigned, if unnatural, loathing for the Yahoos. Though forced to admit their human form, he still thinks himself as not of their 'Species' (IV. ii. 233). This ontological fear, where reason represents that we must be something quite other than what we have been pleased to suppose we were, has already been touched on in Part II. In Part IV it takes on an altogether more dire and dramatic form.

It is now right to consider Gulliver's new masters, the Houyhnhnms, who by the beginning of chapter 3, have found out what Gulliver likes to eat and drink, and decided to give him shelter. Gulliver quickly learns the simple hierarchy of this Houyhnhnm household. The Dapple-Grey neighs with authority, and is soon referred to as 'the Master Horse' or even 'his Honour'; the Sorrel Nag, which is a smaller horse of a red-brown colour, is his servant and valet. Beneath the equine servants are the Yahoos: Gulliver sees four of them drawing an elderly Houyhnhnm in a sledge (IV. ii. 233). Gulliver's first impression of the horses as orderly and rational is borne out by experience, and from the first they treat him gently and with consideration. They are civil and decorous with one another, shaking hoofs on meeting and parting, living in simple and clean accommodation, enjoying a plain diet, their mares decent and their colts and foals modest. 'Houyhnhnm', Gulliver learns, means both horse and, originally, *perfection of Nature* (IV. iii. 237). His master, the Dapple-Grey, is filled with impatience and curiosity for Gulliver to learn the Houyhnhnm tongue, so that more may be discovered about this strange creature and the world he comes from. This is an important moral sign in *Gulliver's Travels*. Neither the Emperor of Lilliput nor the King of Laputa were curious about Gulliver or his world. The King of Brobdingnag and the Houyhnhnm master, on the other hand, show the real humanist's eagerness to learn from strange experience.

It may be noted that Part IV is the only place in a narrative of so many wonderful countries where Gulliver doubts his senses, and resorts to the notion of enchantment. A talking and rational horse he finds utterly incredible. If the Houyhnhnms are to seem rational and benevolent, as Gulliver has so far found them, why does Swift choose horses as his rational and benevolent beings? Involved in his choice is first of all a pleasant academic joke, first pointed out by R.S. Crane in a notable essay, 'The Houyhnhnms, the Yahoos, and the History of Ideas'. From the third-century AD philosopher Porphyry on, thinkers seeking to distinguish man from other animals by his reason gave the horse as an example of the other animals: animals without reason. This Porphyrian formulation was perpetuated in the logic textbooks of the seventeenth and eighteenth centuries, including those prescribed at Trinity College Dublin when Swift was there, above all in Narcissus Marsh's *Institutio Logicae* (1679). From such exercises the undergraduate came away with his mind full of vulnerably unexamined commonplaces (their purpose was, after all, not to inculcate truths but to illustrate modes of argument). Chief among such commonplaces was the proposition that man is an animal; that a horse is also an animal; but that man only has the property of reason (*animal rationale*) while the horse only has the property of whinnying (*animal hinnibile*). Swift has taken a commonplace, even a *cliché*, of serious original implication, and provokingly turned it upside down. The whole fable of the Houyhnhnms and Yahoos in Part IV appears to rest on this humorous, mocking and provocative reversal.

In taking this opportunity, however, Swift also remembered the various and important rôles of the horse in history and society. These ranged from being an object of power and terror (the warhorse in a cavalry charge), to being a costly sign of high social rank (a handsome, well-bred, animal for riding, hunting, or harnessing to a splendid carriage), a trustworthy and indispensable means of travelling (a reliable sorrel nag, perhaps), a source of energy to pull the plough and farm cart and, as Gulliver will in due course honestly acknowledge to the Dapple-Grey, to being creatures 'used to all kind of Drudgery till they died; after which their Skins were stripped and sold for what they were worth, and their bodies left to be devoured by Dogs and Birds of Prey' (IV.iv.243). To this range of social use, mythological and literary associations should be added. Remembering perhaps the mettlesome but disciplined steed ridden by Virgil in Swift's *Battle of the Books*, Pope had used the traditional image of the horse in *An Essay on Criticism* (1711):

> 'Tis more to *guide* than *spur* the Muse's Steed;
> Restrain his Fury, than provoke his Speed;
> The winged Courser, like a gen'rous Horse,
> Shows most true Mettle when you *check* his Course.
>
> (lines 84–7)

In selecting horses to embody qualities opposite to those which Gulliver saw in the Yahoos, Swift chose a creature which could potentially express inspiration, eloquence, nobility, strength, friendliness, familiarity, service, and value even when dead and delivered to the knacker's yard. The text of Part IV plays on all these associations to some degree, but perhaps the note most often struck is that of domestic familiarity.

At this point the literary genre of the beast fable must be briefly recalled. Swift was familiar with this form. He had mocked (and probably learned from) Dryden's beast fable, *The Hind and the Panther* (1687), and in his own *Battle of the Books* the confrontation of the spider and the bee had been moralized by none other than Aesop. The art of the beast fable, it may be thought, requires a nice combination of knowledge of animal behaviour, and of the human qualities which can playfully but instructively be attributed to animals. Chaucer's *Nonne's Priest's Tale*, modernized by Dryden in his *Fables*, is a prime example. There is real humour involved in this quasi-pastoral juxtaposing of man and beast. The humour of Swift's treatment of the Houyhnhnms, in Part IV, and even of the Yahoos, should be remembered, for it gives light, shade and subtlety to what would otherwise seem a starkly polarized fiction. Two horses courteously shaking hoofs, a stallion and a mare showing themselves 'extremely chearful and complaisant' to their guest at supper while 'the young colt and fole appeared very modest', the 'Decency and Regularity' with which each horse and mare 'eat their own Hay, and their own Mash of Oats and Milk', the picture of the 'white Mare of our Family' threading a needle by using the hollow part of the fore-foot between pastern and hoof (p. 280), the extravagant Yahoos who manage to dig shining stones out of the earth and hide them, 'but still looking round with great Caution, for fear their Comrades should find out their Treasure' (IV. vii. 265): such details seem far from any desperate dispute about the nature and adequacy of reason in human life, though Part IV certainly opens up this dispute. Rather they remind us of that childlike but telling capacity to see human qualities in familiar animals, so that foxes are cunning, cocks vainglorious, dogs faithful, cats superior, and so forth.

A further and connected point becomes clear as we reflect on the early scenes of Gulliver in the land of the Houyhnhnms. While Parts III and IV do not contrast so obviously as Parts I and II, they contrast significantly none the less. Part III is full of artifice: the successful applied science of the flying island, the misconceived projects of Lagado, the treacherous artifice of some of the political projectors. The fuller than usual description of the island from which Gulliver was rescued by Laputa implicitly enforces this point. On this island, 'all rocky, only a little intermingled with Tufts of Grass, and sweet smelling Herbs', with birds' eggs, dried seaweed and parched grass (III. i. 152), Gulliver could have survived by the means nature afforded, before the great loadstone drew the flying island between him and the sun. Now, in Part IV, the Houyhnhnms seem to live a similarly simple and natural life, in what is in many respects a pastoral world.

It is within this world, with its simple agricultural economy and the warm absurdity of its beast-fable life, that Swift now introduces the most extended Utopian conversation in the *Travels*. The word conversation is used advisedly, for what now follows is a brilliant new evolution from More's work. There, Hythloday, though participating in a dialogue with his fellow Europeans, simply describes the kingdom of Utopia: 'they say', 'they have', 'they set great store', 'they marvel' – these expressions and their like form the idiom of his account. This is Gulliver's own idiom in the 'miniature Utopia' of Part I, chapter 6. In Part II, however, Swift introduces a variation.

Gulliver delivers an oration in praise of Europe while the King of Brobdingnag takes notes; Gulliver is then subject to cross-examination, and made to listen to the King's withering condemnation. This is a lot more dramatic than the simple description of an ideal commonwealth. Nevertheless it has the structured formality of an audience with a king. Here in Part IV Gulliver has conversations with the Dapple-Grey, beset by linguistic and cultural difficulty, full of interruption and misunderstanding, and with a variety of emotions suffusing the discourse.

Apart from his as yet imperfect mastery of the hinnibilian tongue, for example, Gulliver has great difficulty in explaining what a ship is, and how it can be propelled by wind – a technological stage much behind that of Laputa. Even when a physical account is clear, a natural Houyhnhnm misunderstanding can arise which continues beast-fable comedy into Utopian discussion:

When I asserted that the *Yahoos* were the only governing Animals in my Country, which my Master said was altogether past his Conception, he desired to know, whether we had *Houyhnhnms* among us, and what was their Employment: I told him, we had great Numbers; that in Summer they grazed in the Fields, and in Winter were kept in Houses, with Hay and Oats, where *Yahoo*-servants were employed to rub their Skins smooth, comb their Manes, pick their Feet, serve them with Food, and make their Beds. I understand you well, said my Master; it is now very plain from all you have spoken, that whatever Share of Reason the *Yahoos* pretend to, the *Houyhnhnms* are your Masters; I heartily wish our *Yahoos* would be so tractable.

(IV. iv. 242–3)

In this last remark the tones of some European master talking of the difficulty of getting good servants are unmistakable. Gulliver has, of course, to plough on with his hard task of making the Dapple-Grey understand the true situation of Houyhnhnms in Europe.

During the early discussions the reader notices a vein of honesty, or perhaps realism, in Gulliver which had not been obvious in his presentation of his own world in Part II. For example he tells the Dapple-Grey roundly that he left his native land ('governed by a Female Man, whom we called a *Queen*')

'to get Riches' and, the subject of vice having been raised by
mention of his mutinous crew, develops this into a fuller
discourse in which 'I endeavoured to give him some Ideas of
the Desire of Power and Riches; of the terrible Effects of Lust,
Intemperance, Malice, and Envy. All this I was forced to
define and describe by putting Cases and making Suppositions'
(IV. iv. 246). This is far from the attitude adopted by Gulliver
in Part II: he is no longer eager to sing the praises of 'our noble
Country, the Mistress of Arts and Arms, the Scourge of France'
(II. iii. 99). While the King of Brobdingnag's condemnations
provoked in Gulliver an indignant and aggressive response,
Gulliver now reacts very differently to the equally telling
judgements of the Dapple-Grey. There is, however, one significant exception. When the Houyhnhnm points out that, however
irrationally the Europeans resort to war, 'Nature hath left
you utterly uncapable of doing such Mischief', Gulliver is
stung by this physical contempt, and reacts in his gunpowder
mood which the reader recalls from Part II:

I could not forbear shaking my Head and smiling a little at his
Ignorance. And, being no Stranger to the Art of War, I gave him a
Description of Cannons, Culverins, Muskets, Carabines, Pistols,
Bullets, Powder, Swords, Bayonets, Sieges, Retreats, Attacks, Under-
mines, Countermines, Bombardments, Sea-fights; Ships sunk with a
Thousand Men; twenty Thousand killed on each Side; Dying Groans,
Limbs flying in the Air: Smoak, Noise, Confusion, trampling to
Death under Horses Feet: Flight, Pursuit, Victory; Fields strewed
with Carcases left for Food to Dogs, and Wolves, and Birds of Prey;
Plundering, Stripping, Ravishing, Burning and Destroying. And, to
set forth the Valour of my own dear Country-men ...   (IV. v. 250−1)

This passage is among the more characteristically powerful of
the *Travels*. Opening a paragraph, the short first sentence, the
brevity of which seems to convey the inadequacy of Gulliver's
opening judgement, is succeeded by a very long sentence (nine
and a half lines to one and a half, the whole paragraph being
concluded by one of four and a half) which invokes one of the
famous formal topics of the Renaissance, 'the Art of War',
the subject of numerous treatises including one by Machiavelli.
The same sentence immediately follows up with one of Swift's
outrageously prolonged lists, in which it is shown how 'the Art

of War' resolves into no more than a recitation of kinds of weapon (nine of them) and types of tactic (seven of them). Single terms give way to more elaborated expressions ('Ships sunk with a Thousand Men' & c.) as Swift turns to the effects of 'the Art of War', and, as the long sentence nears its end, a faster alternation of brevity with extension is achieved, 'Flight, Pursuit, Victory' contrasting with 'Fields strewed with Carcases left for Food to Dogs ...'. The sentence plunges down to the logical conclusion of this modern art of war with a final devastating succession of single words: 'Plundering, Stripping, Ravishing, Burning and Destroying.' The emergence of sexual violence in this list between 'Plundering' and 'Burning' should not be ignored. The third and final sentence of the paragraph brilliantly reintroduces the complacent and patriotic Gulliver whom the reader has perhaps temporarily forgotten. The same instinctive psychology is now noticed in Gulliver as was found in his final conversations with the King in Part II. The use of Gulliver as a satiric device is somehow enveloped by a simple continuous character. His view may change with circumstance and, perhaps, experience, but some of his reactions remain the same. At this particular point the Dapple-Grey cuts him off imperiously, and changes the subject from war to law.

We are made well aware of the striking change in Gulliver's attitude to his own world. Perhaps because, having learned the Houyhnhnm language, he sees himself very much the active instructor, struggling to make the simple and rational horse perceive the dreadful complexities of Europe, and assuming a kind of pedagogical authority, Gulliver describes his society as he now believes it to be. Having revealed the dreadful facts of war, almost by an instinct of self-assertion, he deliberately and unhesitatingly exposes the legal and medical professions. When he comes to speak of politicians the reader is reminded, first, of the few awful examples Gulliver had communicated to the political projectors in Part III, secondly and in contrast, of his panegyric on British institutions in Part II, thirdly and now more remotely, of his deadpan account of Chancellor Flimnap on the tightrope in Part I. The description of the chief minister in Part IV suggests that Gulliver has come a long way:

a Creature wholly exempt from Joy and Grief, Love and Hatred, Pity and Anger; at least makes use of no other Passions but a violent Desire of Wealth, Power, and Titles: That he applies his Words to all Uses, except to the Indication of his Mind; that he never tells a *Truth*, but with an Intent that you should take it for a *Lye*; nor a *Lye*, but with a Design that you should take it for a *Truth*; That those he speaks worst of behind their Backs, are in the surest way to Preferment; and whenever he begins to praise you to others or to your self, you are from that Day forlorn.   (IV. vi. 259)

This passage was prefaced, in the first edition, by an account of how Queen Anne rules without relying on any particular minister, having no interest to serve save the good of her subjects (*Works*, xi. 318), an implicit criticism of George I who did just the opposite. It focuses on Robert Walpole, or some one very like him, and not only delivers an honest and severe judgement on current political life, but is admirably calculated to contrast with the practice of the Houyhnhnms, for whom the circumlocution '*the thing which was not*' was necessary to convey that difficult notion, a lie (IV. iii. 237). The sophisticated corruption of the '*Chief Minister*', who can tell a truth in order to deceive, is almost impossibly remote, morally, from the plain and simple life of the Houyhnhnms. This passage contains a penetrating and powerful analysis, and can hardly help but persuade the reader to trust the person who utters it. Soon Gulliver himself comments on his new candour, and does so in such a way as to fortify our sense of his continuity through the four parts of the *Travels*:

THE READER may be disposed to wonder how I could prevail on my self to give so free a Representation of my own Species, among a Race of Mortals who were already too apt to conceive the vilest Opinion of Human Kind, from that entire Congruity betwixt me and their *Yahoos*. But I must freely confess, that the many Virtues of those excellent *Quadrupeds* placed in opposite View to human Corruptions, had so far opened mine Eyes, and enlarged my Understanding, that I began to view the Actions and Passions of Man in a very different Light; and to think the Honour of my own Kind not worth managing ...

He goes on to record his 'firm Resolution' to live among the Houyhnhnms for good, contemplating their virtues, and protected from any incitement to vice, and this is another reason for the frankness of his account. However, he adds retrospectively, it is some comfort that he '*extenuated*' the faults of his countrymen by giving them 'as *favourable* a Turn as the Matter would bear' (IV. vii. 262–3) so far as possible. This last remark lends an irony indeed, after such tremendous condemnations: it also clearly reminds of that other, earlier occasion, when Gulliver gave a 'favourable turn' to his account, speaking of Britain to the King of Brobdingnag (II. vii. 127). This is manifestly the same Gulliver, with the same instinct: in Part II the 'favourable turn' helps support a naive panegyric; in Part IV it makes his condemnations (if conceivable) even more severe.

If, but only if, we assume some continuity of character in Gulliver, his conversion to honest pessimism about his own world, though a striking moral evolution, may not be accepted without a touch of misgiving by the alert reader. Leaving aside the panegyrical Gulliver of Part II, the reader may recall the deferential Gulliver of the early chapters of Part I, and wonder whether his present straightforward admiration of the Houyhnhnms will not in due course require some reassessment. Further, admire the Houyhnhnms as he may, Gulliver's sudden disclosure in chapter 7 that he now thought of staying with them indefinitely does prompt a question about those 'dear Pledges', his family at Redriff, whom he has often spoken of during his earlier voyages. For example in a poignant moment early in Part II, Gulliver fell asleep 'and dreamed I was at home with my Wife and Children, which aggravated my Sorrows when I awaked and found myself alone in a vast Room ...' (II. i. 83). Where has that comforting dream gone now? Can Gulliver be wholly in possession of the experience upon which so important a human decision ought to be based?

His argument, of course, is his gratitude to the Dapple-Grey and admiration for the Houyhnhnms, and it is now time to turn from Gulliver's new view of his own world, gradually evolving as we may suppose it to have been in the later chapters of part III, to his high esteem for the rational horses, whose way of life in its moral and political aspects is the chief focus of attention in the later chapters of Part IV.

The Dapple-Grey shows both tact and kindness to his anomalous guest. Though convinced that he must be a Yahoo of some kind (confirmed when Gulliver is seen without his clothes, first by the Sorrel Nag, later by a female Yahoo), the Houyhnhnm is more than ready to make an exception in this interesting case. In the wonderful conversations between him and Gulliver he is more innocent, and therefore less of a moralist, than the King of Brobdingnag who ruled an imperfect people and knew human nature only too well. The Dapple-Grey, by contrast, finds it hard to see the point of being vicious (IV. iv. 246); he plainly thinks war to be irrational though his opinion is masked in a simple irony (IV. v. 250); and he assumes that 'all Animals' − a phrase which must include Yahoos − have 'a Title to their Share in the Productions of the Earth; and especially those who presided over the rest' (IV. vi. 255). He thinks in terms of rank, observing some natural distinctions in appearance and capacity among the Houyhnhnms, and wonders whether Gulliver's difference from the rest of the Yahoos might not be because he has some tincture of noble blood. His grand conclusion from all Gulliver's communications − comparable to the King of Brobdingnag's 'little odious Vermin' speech − is 'That our Institutions of *Government* and *Law* were plainly owing to our gross Defects in *Reason*, and by consequence in Virtue; because Reason alone is sufficient to govern a *Rational* Creature ...' (IV. vii. 263). He drives his point home by drawing several parallels between the behaviour of the Yahoos and what Gulliver has told him about his own fellow creatures.

Gulliver's own summary account of the Houyhnhnms, which harks back to the simpler Utopian narrative of Hythloday, stresses that reason among them, though needing to be cultivated, is neither discursive, nor persuasive, nor directed to the creation of totalizing rational structures: 'it is what strikes you with immediate Conviction ...' (IV. viii. 273). Friendship, Benevolence, Decency and Civility are their virtues, and 'Nature teaches them to love the whole Species ...'. In marriage choice they consider genetic balance rather than love or material interest, and such marriages are never violated. Their young are raised to be hardy and athletic, but, in balance to this emphasis on physical prowess, victors in athletic contests are rewarded, as in Pindar, with 'a Song made in his or her Praise' (IV. viii. 275). Their culture is oral, like that of Homer, and 'In *Poetry* they must be allowed to excel all other Mortals; wherein the justness of their Similes, and the Minuteness, as well as Exactness of their Descriptions, are indeed inimitable' (IV. ix. 280). They live to about seventy or seventy-five and do not fear death. To appreciate their composed and practical attitude to the termination of experience, it is only necessary to recall the doom of the immortal Struldbruggs in Part III. Politically the Houyhnhnms are primitive republicans. They are governed by a Council of their whole nation which meets every four years for a period of five or six days. This settles questions of rural economy, of marriages, and of the only matter of debate 'that ever happened in their Country': the Yahoo question (IV. ix. 277).

It is the Yahoo question which brings Gulliver to grief. For the first and only time on these voyages he has found happiness. He has a good hut, makes his own clothes, and lives on a simple diet. Free from the temptations and treacheries of Europe (among which in one of his great lists of ills he includes 'ranting, lewd, expensive wives' − IV. x. 284) he enjoys health of body, peace of mind, and good conversation. Meanwhile the Assembly, reviewing the question of the Yahoos once again, and the pros and cons of exterminating them, considers the possibilities of a systematic programme of castration, a notion which the Dapple-Grey has borrowed from Gulliver's mention of the castration of horses in Europe (IV. iv. 244, IV. ix. 279). The Yahoos had not, according to legend, always been in the country of the Houyhnhnms, were not very good workers, and it would be better to cultivate asses instead. In the light of all this, the Dapple-Grey's strange Yahoo, tinctured with reason, poses a particular problem. It is argued that he should either be treated like the rest of the Yahoos, or be made to swim home, since it is 'not agreeable to Reason or Nature' for a Houyhnhnm to keep a Yahoo in his family (IV. x. 286). It is then recognized that the partly rational Yahoo might be capable of leading a revolt of the Yahoos against their masters. Gulliver must therefore be expelled. The thoughful Dapple-Grey suggests that Gulliver may be able to construct a craft by which to reach his native land. Gulliver swoons with shock and grief and, on his recovery, expresses his feelings in what is for Part IV a rare Gulliverian irony: '... in my weak and corrupt Judgement, I thought it might consist with Reason to have been less rigorous. That I could not swim a League ...' (IV. x. 287).

The exhortation of the Assembly cannot, however, be disputed, though the kindly Dapple-Grey would have kept Gulliver in his service as long as he lived (IV. x. 287). The Sorrel Nag helps Gulliver make a canoe of Yahoo skins (the reader here recalls Gulliver's earlier mention of how horse skins are sold for use in Europe − IV. iv. 243), Gulliver makes his *adieux* weeping and with a heart 'sunk with Grief', pushes off into the sea, and the Sorrel Nag '(who always loved me)' cries out 'Take care of thy self, gentle Yahoo', as tide and wind carry him away.

Only now, with the fable of Part IV before us, are we in a position to consider the longest-running Swiftian controversy of the twentieth century: the question of the author's meaning in his presentation of the Houyhnhnms. Are they offered for our admiration as Gulliver admires them, or are they, possibly, a satire on reason, as the Yahoos seem to be a satire on the appetites? The first reaction of Swift's own generation was to find in the Houyhnhnms and Yahoos delightfully provocative comedy. But by 1752, at the latest, the whole issue had become vexed, as may be seen from Lord Orrery's *Remarks on the Life and Writings of Dr Jonathan Swift*. One of Swift's younger friends, Orrery writes on Part IV as if it were a severe sermon he has had to hear from Swift more than once, and is resolved to repudiate. All awareness of comedy is gone, Swift's picture of the Houyhnhnms is 'cold and insipid', and the whole Houyhnhnm/Yahoo contrast is rejected as not being a fair way of thinking about human nature. Orrery has no doubt about Swift's *intentions* in Part IV: they are 'to indulge a misanthropy that is intolerable' (Williams, *Heritage*, 126−7). The unwelcome challenge of Part IV is thus read directly back

into the character of Swift in his later years, designated misanthropy, and henceforth treated as 'a case', a problem of
moral psychology. This was, on the whole, how the nineteenth
century would cope with whatever it found uncomfortable in
the writings of Swift.

Once a more formalistic critical mode was established, and
readers became wary of identifying Swift with Gulliver, a new
way of evading the discomfort of Part IV became available.
If Gulliver were sometimes the object of Swift's satire, for
example at the end of Part II, might he not be the object of a
subtler and more profound satire in Part IV? Might not the
entire Houyhnhnm/Yahoo polarity be a moral and psychological trap into which the unsuspecting Gulliver falls, and
the reader with him? This hypothesis rests primarily on the
proposition that Swift himself did not consider human beings
to be rational animals, and, secondly, on the existence of certain
deistic utopias within the recent tradition of fictional voyages.
Implying the redundancy of revelation, redemption, and special
providence, such works seemed to endorse the recognition
of whatever divinity the harmony of Nature disclosed. The
Houyhnhnm insistence on reason, it was argued, signalled a
Swiftian satire on deistic utopias. This view was heavily but-
tressed by repetitions of what Orrery first asserted: that the
Houyhnhnms are 'cold and insipid' and that we, Swift's readers,
do not like them. In this interpretation the comedy of the
Houyhnhnms (a mare threading a needle, &c.), far from
domesticating rationality, becomes ridicule of reason.

It certainly is true that Swift did not think that humankind
were rational animals. Behind his teasing reversal of the man/
horse distinction is the view he expressed in a famous letter
to Pope, 29 September 1725, that he had 'got Materials Towards
a Treatis proving the falsity of that Definition *animal rationale*;
and to show it should be only *rationis capax*': man is not
rational but only capable of reason. 'Upon this great foundation
of Misanthropy ... The whole building of my Travells is
erected ...' (*Correspondence*, III. 103). If we are not wholly
rational, however, it does not follow that we are wrong to
admire reason, nor, if we are capable of reason, that a rational

example may not be valuable to us. Further, the argument about deistic utopias is quite unconvincing. Emphasis on the sufficiency of reason for rational creatures does not become deism unless revelation is formally repudiated (G. Douglas Atkins, 'Pope and Deism'). The Houyhnhnms never mention Revelation; neither, for that matter do the Emperor of Lilliput, the King of Brobdingnag, or the King of Laputa. As we have seen, Christianity itself has no explicit rôle in the *Travels*, though a scatter of minor references by Gulliver tells us that it should not be forgotten. Where the Yahoos are concerned, the notion that Swift's presentation of them is ironically repellent, a trap for Gulliver and the reader, has to cope with Swift's letter to the Reverend Thomas Sheridan, of 11 September 1725, where he advises his younger friend to 'expect no more from Man than such an Animal is capable of, and you will every day find my Description of Yahoos more resembling'. Swift goes on to advise Sheridan: 'You should think and deal with every Man as a Villain, without calling him so, or flying from him, or valuing him less.' (*Correspondence*, III.94). Of course the Yahoos are designed to shock and provoke. But there are no good reasons for thinking them anything other than a powerful satire on a race of creatures who, while capable of reason, are chiefly driven by instinct and desire. As for the remaining arguments, they are widely attractive because they are too easy. They rest on a belated, neo-Romantic cult of feeling, anachronistic when applied to Swift, uncritical in regard to ourselves. This line of interpretation of Part IV has been effectively disposed of by the best living critic of Swift, Claude Rawson, in his book, *Gulliver and the Gentle Reader*. If, however, two facile ways of dismissing Swift's vision have eventually been exposed, what remain for serious readers are the difficulties which Swift knowingly leaves behind. The Country of the Houyhnhnms is, for Gulliver, a peaceful refuge from the maelstrom of appetite, murky or murderous, which life in Europe now means for him. Far from 'cold and insipid', the Dapple-Grey is tentative if reasonable, kindly if rational, tactful if plainspeaking, often moved by understandable emotion, a being whose exemplary and comic rôles complement rather than subvert one another: 'his Honour' wonders why the European Houyhnhnms don't throw their Yahoo riders and, by rolling on them, squeeze the brutes to death (IV. iv. 243). 'Brutes', a word often used by the Houyhnhnms of the Yahoos, is a strong word, meaning an animal without mind or soul, yet the picture of the wilful horse rolling on its rider, dangerous enough, indeed, to a poor jockey, manages to familiarise the powers of pure reason.

The Dapple-Grey, however, is overruled by the Assembly, few members of which know Gulliver as well as he does. As for the Assembly's overall design, it is an excellent example of rational self-interest, directed to the ends of the convenience and prosperity of the Houyhnhnms. Such a goal takes no account of the emotional and rational nature of Gulliver, nor indeed of the other Yahoos who, if Gulliver can grow more rational, might do so too. The reader should not, however, make the mistake of generalizing the Houyhnhnms. The personal kindness and wisdom of the Dapple-Grey, overruled by the public Assembly, is something sufficiently familiar in the human world to preclude accusations of comprehensive, unfeeling rationality.

But the Houyhnhnms are Utopian. More's text admitted reservations about the Utopian commonwealth, the rôle of which was, perhaps, less to offer a model for total imitation, than an example to show that things as they were might certainly be changed. So it is with the Houyhnhnms. It is interesting how often Utopian commonwealths come to depend on apparently lesser beings. Plato's Republic assumes the institution of slavery; More's Utopians make good use of the Zapoletes, a race of thieves and hunters only fit for war. The Houyhnhnms, like More's Utopians, put an (allegedly) inferior race to use, while still wishing to wipe it out. These fictions surely say a great deal about idealistic totalitarianism. Even in the guise of beast–fable comedy the ideality of the Houyhnhnms can be frightening. Their proposal in their Assembly to 'exterminate all the brutes' (see Joseph Conrad, *Heart of Darkness*, II) draws a genetic line which the unpredictable rhetorical and moral mobility of Swift's text never endorses. Furthermore, to the degree that we envisage Gulliver as a character, we begin to imagine how much the sense of his being appreciated as an *exceptional* Yahoo, on the right side of the line, must confirm him in his esteem for his new masters. (Racial and meritocratic analogues from later times are not far to seek.) And in the end the Houyhnhnms as Utopians are frightening, not because their reason is a sufficient guide to rational creatures, and therefore of no relevance to us *animalia rationis capacia*; but, because we are *rationis capax*, their example could be of relevance to us. Thus the dizzying gulf between reason and reality remains, and Gulliver, behind the hapless comedy of his misadventures, is in a tragic conflict: reasonable enough to want to live with reason, never rational enough for reason to be a sufficient rule of his life; pledged, furthermore, to the lives of other partly reasonable beings back in England, lives which he has temporarily forgotten.

Chapter 8

Concluding

This delicate balance of assessment, this double vision, is of course affected by the reader's response to the two final chapters which Swift has given us of the *Travels*. Will it be a fine day, a fine day in the end? If there is one point on which modern commentators are agreed in their consideration of Gulliver, it is the kind character of Don Pedro de Mendez, the Portuguese Sea Captain, whose ship eventually picks Gulliver up and takes him home to Europe. The reason we warm to Don Pedro so willingly may have something to do with the similar rôle of Glumdalclitch in Part II, who knew no more of what and where Gulliver had been than Don Pedro, but who speedily saw his difficulties, and helped him with instinctive love to adjust to the terrible physical proportions of Brobdingnag. Don Pedro, it is often said, is one of those minor but significant individuals in Swift, of whom, though he may 'hate and detest that animal called man', he can say things like: 'I hartily love John, Peter, Thomas and so forth' (*Correspondence*, III. 103). However, further distinctions need to be made among these rare, minor, good figures in the *Travels*. Secretary Reldresal, for example, consistently represented as Gulliver's friend in Lilliput, in the end only achieves the political compromise that Gulliver shall be blinded and starved to death. Reldresal may have been Gulliver's friend but he was not an effective one. Glumdalclitch, on the other hand, a little girl whose pet lamb had recently been taken away from her to the slaughter, doted on Gulliver first as a new pet, but soon loved him as a mother might love a precocious child. Lord Munodi, in Part III, is not called on to help Gulliver, but his encounter with him is a sad and touching meeting of minds in a good place that is unlikely to survive. Less can be said about the Sorrel Nag than any of these. His astonishment at discovering Gulliver metamorphosed, that is partly unclothed, is simple and comic: right at the end, after he has helped Gulliver build his canoe, the reader hears, in parenthesis, that this horse always loved him. He calls him 'gentle Yahoo' because his picture of Gulliver is based on how the latter has behaved in the country of the Houyhnhnms, while the Dapple-Grey has heard Gulliver's not invariably gentle sentiments. Gulliver treats the Dapple-Grey as a great noble who honours him with his civilities; the rôle of the Sorrel Nag, on the other hand, is to show how the new Gulliver is grateful for the love even of a lowly equine servant. These comparisons bring out the great importance of Don Pedro de Mendes, an exceptionally humane, patient and effective helper, whom Gulliver for long enough treats quite abominably. To use some of Gulliver's own words, 'it might consist with Reason' to show a little more gratitude. This, I think, is Swift's final, dramatic *volte-face*, by which sympathy with a Gulliver expelled by the very beings he admires is superseded by a much less favourable opinion. This attitude is fortified when we see how Gulliver treats his wife and family on his final return to Redriff. It should now be clear that the art of *Gulliver's Travels* is, in great measure, an art of altering viewpoint and assessment in which the Four Parts, far from being merely four separate forays into satire, are complementary and bound together in a coherent rhetorical strategy aimed at the reader. To summarize and simplify, in Part I Gulliver wins our approval. We trust him, therefore, at the beginning of Part II, are inclined to identify with him, and thus receive with him the full force of the King of Brobdingnag's giant judgements. We can here only distance ourselves from Gulliver and, were we to have moved straight to Part IV, we should, I think, have distrusted him ever after. But as Swift finally shaped his *Travels* Part III intervenes, during the course of which Gulliver is gradually edged back into our sympathy. The reader is thus much closer to Gulliver as he experiences loathing for the Yahoos, admiration for the Houyhnhnms, and the painful conflict about the nature of his very being. In no major satirical work of Swift is the reader allowed to sit back, exempt from the follies and dilemmas which his fictions obtrude. So it is here.

Lured a second time into near-identification with Gulliver, the reader is again confronted with a most embarrassing and painful need for self-assessment and moral adjustment. This is the Swiftian experience *par excellence*: it depends not on a Gulliver who merely comprises four separate satiric *personae*, but one who has continuity of character from Part to Part. Swift's art within the changing relationship between Gulliver and the reader − an art which has something in common with viewpoint in Henry James and Conrad − is, I think, one of our major critical recognitions as we draw to the end of the *Travels*.

There are two others, however, each of high interest. The first concerns the absent God of this strange work by an energetic Christian churchman. By comparison with Dampier and Defoe, not to mention the seventeenth-century collections of Purchas, the *Travels* is not only remarkably silent about the Christian faith, but, at those moments at which a conventional eighteenth-century reader would most expect Gulliver to say something Christian, whether a prayer of petition or an effusion of thanks, Gulliver does not do so. Indeed, he usually says something pointedly opposite. 'We therefore trusted ourselves to the Mercy of the Waves ... I swam as Fortune directed me ...' (I. i. 5); 'condemned by Nature and Fortune ...' (II. i. 73); 'wholly overcome by Grief and Despair ... But my good Star would have it ...' (II. i. 76−8); my evil Destiny so ordered ...' (II. viii. 145); 'In this desolate Condition I advanced forward ...' (IV. i. 225): these are the expressions Gulliver uses to describe moments of crisis and danger, or new settings out. If we look for moments of thanksgiving to God for deliverance or safe arrival home, we shall not find any. In Part IV there is, indeed, a moment when Gulliver falls on his knees. He does so 'to preserve my Liberty' and beg that he may not be rescued by the Yahoo Pedro de Mendes and his crew (IV. xi. 294−5). We draw the same conclusion. At the most important moments of his life Gulliver appears to be a man without religion. This is a salient difference from the chief English predecessors of the *Travels*. Should we then read the *Travels* as a completely secular work in an increasingly secular age? Problems would at once arise concerning both age and author to check such an hypothesis. Eighteenth-century England was probably not growing more secular, nor does this seem to have been the case with Swift in his other writings. In any case, the text of the *Travels* itself will not allow us to forget the matter of Christianity. Gulliver may not pray to God in crisis as Dampier did, or thank God for deliverance like Crusoe, but, in Part I, in Gulliver's draft Utopia on Lilliput, he records without comment how the Lilliputians are buried upside down so as to ensure (given the ultimate revolution of the Lilliputians' flat earth) that they will be standing at the resurrection and how, in the Lilliputian state, 'the Disbelief of a Divine Providence renders a Man uncapable of holding any publick Station' (I. vi. 47). The first allusion gave offence to his younger contemporaries (Delaney, *Observations*) though it was no more than a ridicule on the kind of literalistic religion satirized in Hall's *Mundus Alter et Idem*. The second reference has about it the air of a rationalized Test Act (legislation, supported by Swift, requiring commitment to the Established Church before holding public office). Neither reference tells us much about Gulliver, but each reminds us of an essential feature of Swift's religion and that of the overwhelming majority of his readership: belief in the resurrection of the body and in a special providence through the operation of the Holy Spirit. These allusions, placed early in the *Travels* and in a situation which appears somewhat dislocated from human practice, quietly remind of a Christian standard by which Gulliver could be judged, if the reader thought fit. The fact that these details occur in the Utopian sequence of Part I suggests that Gulliver himself would not come all that well out of such a Christian assessment. Gulliver is, however, at least a nominal Christian. So much emerges, as we have seen, from his refusal to trample on the crucifix in Japan. It can hardly be an accident that this episode follows directly on that awful example of immortal mortality, the Struldbruggs. Gulliver himself, characteristically, makes no connection. Gulliver's later reference to eucharistic and other religious disputes in his conversations with the Dapple-Grey is casual and dismissive (IV. v. 249).

Then, near the end of Part IV, Gulliver is, in terms of his own vision of things, obliged to descend from a realm of wisdom, reason, virtue and peace, to a fallen land of appetite, ambition, destruction and self-destruction. Gulliver's vision may be right, or wrong, or half-right (Swift teases us with a paradoxical double vision) but there can be no doubt that this is, or ought to be, some kind of evangelical situation. After all, the Dapple-Grey in his willingness to keep Gulliver, and even the doctrinaire Houyhnhnm Assembly in its decision to expel him, acknowledge the possibility that Yahoos have it in them to change. Yet Gulliver who so admires the Houyhnhnms will not draw this moral and apply it to the Yahoos of his native land. Behind and above the missionary opportunity that any Christian might see is, of course, the crux of the Christian creed, Christ as the Word become Flesh, or, in the 'comfortable words' of the Book of Common Prayer that Swift used, 'Christ Jesus came into the world to save sinners' (The Communion; I Timothy, i. 15). The Portuguese sea-captain, not accidentally perhaps called Pedro, or Peter, has the rôle of attempting to assist Gulliver in a descent which might be conceived in a generous light, in distant imitation of Christ. He certainly makes the transition easier for Gulliver, and Lisbon turns out to be less frightful than the latter expects. But Gulliver's thoughts are all for himself. His descent from the Country of the Houyhnhnms to the land of the Yahoos is not a parallel but a pointed anti-parallel to the creed he has nominally professed. We remember More, mentioned by Swift and praised by Gulliver in the Island of the Ghosts. The dialogue between Morus and Hythloday in *Utopia* circled around the questions of whether and how far idealistic practice could be introduced into the ordinary world. Each of them has a clear altruistic intent; and we know that More himself was, at the time of composing *Utopia*, in conflict over whether or not to take high office in England. His decision to do so, thus rejecting Hythloday's all-or-nothing idealism, led in due course to a Christian martyrdom, as Swift knew.

Thanks to Don Pedro, Gulliver reaches Redriff once again. The following two paragraphs (the last of the penultimate chapter of the *Travels*) now repay careful attention.

My Wife and Family received me with great Surprize and Joy, because they had concluded me certainly dead; but I must freely confess, the Sight of them filled me only with Hatred, Disgust and Contempt; and the more, by reflecting on the near Alliance I had to them. For, although since my unfortunate exile from the *Houyhnhnm* Country, I had compelled myself to tolerate the Sight of *Yahoos*, and to converse with Don *Pedro de Mendez*; yet my Memory and Imaginations were perpetually filled with the Virtues and Ideas of those exalted *Houyhnhnms*. And when I began to consider, that by copulating with one of the *Yahoo*-species, I had become a Parent of more; it struck me with the utmost Shame, Confusion and Horror.

As soon as I entered the House, my Wife took me in her Arms, and kissed me; at which, having not been used to the Touch of that odious Animal for so many Years, I fell in a Swoon for almost an Hour. At the Time I am writing, it is five Years since my last Return to *England*: During the first Year I could not endure my Wife or Children in my Presence, the very Smell of them was intolerable; much less could I suffer them to eat in the same Room. To this Hour they dare not presume to touch my Bread, or drink out of the same Cup; neither was I ever able to let one of them take me by the Hand. The first Money I laid out was to buy two young Stone-Horses, which I keep in a good Stable, and next to them the Groom is my greatest Favourite; for I feel my Spirits revived by the Smell he contracts in the Stable. My Horses understand me tolerably well; I converse with them at least four Hours every Day. They are Strangers to Bridle or Saddle; they live in great Amity with me, and Friendship to each other.   (IV. xi. 298)

In a book so full of extraordinary contrast as the *Travels* large allowance may be made for Gulliver's difficulty in adjusting back to life at Redriff. Nevertheless his failure of understanding is obvious: not all Yahoos are the same, and the dreadful and true pictures of Yahoo society at large which Gulliver drew for the Dapple-Grey do not mean that Mrs Gulliver is even partly guilty of all this, let alone an example of what Gulliver had once mentioned in general terms: 'a ranting, lewd and expensive wife'. Some Houyhnhnms could make this kind of distinction; Swift himself could do so; Gulliver cannot. Yahoos are Yahoos for him, though he is a Yahoo himself. The very intensity of Gulliver's moral and physical feeling leads him into mental absolutism.

Swift underlines Gulliver's concluding lack of integrity in various ways. The reader may recall Gulliver's habit, in Parts I and II, of alluding to his family at home as 'dear Pledges' (I. viii. 67) or 'domestick Pledges' (II. viii. 134). This recalls the marriage ceremony in the Book of Common Prayer, where the man declares: 'I plight thee my troth' and the Minister, speaking of the 'covenant' between husband and wife, twice uses the word 'pledge' (or 'pledged') in joining the man and the woman together in Holy Matrimony, 'instituted of God' and 'signifying ... the mystical union that is betwixt Christ and his Church'. One should not to be too solemn about this but, since Gulliver's religion and marriage tend to be neglected topics, it is notable that Gulliver now neglects, or rejects, a great part of what he pledged in his marriage ceremony and, in so doing, forgets a covenant which, in the religion he sometime professed, linked him with God. Next, the three words 'tolerate', 'intolerable' and 'tolerably' demand a brief commentary. They command a wide register of tone and meaning. For example the third instance in this passage ('My horses understand me tolerably well') is the familiar, social, faintly ironic usage, of one who will not consider it good manners to claim too much in a matter of some importance: Gulliver is not so much the Yahoo that his stallions can't understand him. The first instance is totally different. The familiar notion of the tolerable as being somehow an easy matter is quite denied by the paradox of having 'compelled myself to tolerate the sight of *Yahoos*': Swift's choice of words here compels the reader to recall some of the other meanings of the Latin root: to endure, to bear a burden, to support: we are deep into Gulliver's pain here. And that, perhaps, is picked up by the middle word of the three: 'the very Smell of them was intolerable ...' The word 'intolerable' here has a Prayer Book ring, and it will not, shortly, seem a strained connection to recall the words of the general Confession from the Communion Service: 'The remembrance of them [our misdoings] is grievous unto us; The burden of them is intolerable.' In the Prayer Book the misdoings of the sinner are intolerable; for Gulliver it is the smell of his family which is so. But only, of course, because the smell of his family prevents him from forgetting the smell of other sinners, the atrocious deeds of humanity. This sequence of remarks concerning the Book of Common Prayer and its bearing on Gulliver may culminate in what Herbert Davis, the Editor of Swift's *Works*, observed. He noticed the collocation of the words 'presume ... Bread ... Cup' and was rightly reminded of the next stage of the Communion Service after the general Confession: 'We do not presume to come to this thy Table, O merciful Lord, trusting in our own righteousness ...', which continues to speak of the Bread and the Cup that, in the Christian Creed, re-unite man with God. The next clause: 'neither was I ever able to let one of them take me by the Hand' (see Mark, ix. 27; and Turner, p. 377) not only comments on Gulliver's attitude to his family at Redriff but his first encounter with a 'Yahoo': 'The ugly Monster ... approaching nearer, lifted up his fore Paw ...' (IV. i. 226). That, in Part IV, is where Gulliver began to go wrong.

Words and phrases such as these, heard every week by the majority of Swift's readers, finally call our attention to one of the pointed, eloquent, silences in Gulliver's narrative, frequently noted in the foregoing discussion. Gulliver is not secular because the eighteenth century and Swift were sliding into secularism; he is not secular at all, but a nominal, unthinking, Christian, whose formal religion, affirmed at the end of Part III, is no use to him in helping him assess himself, and his judgement of others, in his *Travels Into Several Remote Nations of the World*. The famous fiction of that great ironic Christian Jonathan Swift, shows us how travel can occlude the Creed, and experience be too much for the mind. This is the significance of the difference between Swift, on the one hand, and the more conventional Defoe and Dampier on the other.

A second, connected, issue arises out of the passage quoted above. This concerns Mrs Gulliver, that connective figure, who keeps the home and looks after the family when Gulliver is abroad. In all those practical, circumstantial, realistic, linking passages which tell us of Gulliver's brief homecomings, we hear nothing bad about Gulliver's wife. On the contrary, we hear good (III. i. 149). On Gulliver's final return he is received with surprise and joy, as if he had returned from the dead, and his wife takes him in her arms and kisses him. I conclude that there is a further religious sub-text here, at work indeed in all the English passages in the *Travels*, and activated by the narrator's own name. The surname, Gulliver, a real English name, is obviously chosen by Swift to suggest 'gull', or gull-bearer, the man who bears around with him his own capacity for being well-deceived. But why that unusual Old Testament name Lemuel? Lemuel occurs once only in the Bible, Proverbs, 31, where he is an otherwise unknown king who receives good advice from his mother on women, wine and pity. This advice could have some bearing on Gulliver (for example we have not heard of him drinking wine since it helped him put out the fire in the palace in Lilliput), but what strikes the reader of the *Travels* is the latter part of the chapter in Proverbs which is a famous passage in praise of the good wife. 'Who can find a virtuous woman? For her price is far above rubies. The heart of her husband doth safely trust in her, so that he shall have no need of spoil. She will do him good and not evil all the days of her life ... She openeth her mouth with wisdom; and in her tongue is the law of kindness' (vv. 10–12, 26). Nobody who remembered the one chapter of the Bible which mentioned Lemuel could forget its character of the good wife, which has been Mrs Gulliver's rôle from start to finish. The home has been kept, the family has done well; she has proved worthy of her husband's trust, kept her side of the 'pledge' between them, and never failed to treat him with kindness. Calling Gulliver Lemuel underlines another large area of his experience, relevant to his judgement of his fellow Yahoos, but which has never occupied a lot of his attention, and certainly does not do so on his last return to Redriff. The reader is meant to make a judgement on what Gulliver takes for granted.

In the fable of the spider and the bee, in *The Battle of the Books* (1704), Swift had used Aesop to draw a positive moral from the life of the bee. The battle between the Ancients and the Moderns in which the spider and the bee take sides, is in fact a conflict between two faces of modernity. The spider regards himself as a 'domestic animal', seeing the bee as 'a freebooter over fields and gardens': the bee, seeing himself as 'obliged to Heaven alone for my flights and my music', regards the spider as 'feeding and engendering on itself' in 'a lazy contemplation of four inches round'. The spider is stationary, spinning a flimsy system out of itself; the bee is a rover bringing home honey and wax. The spider trusts in his own self-suffiency; the bee is a mental traveller who discovers new experience, and makes it of value by 'much study, true judgement, and distinction of things'. This distinction is drawn by Aesop himself, in Swift's *Battle*, who dubs the spider the 'Modern' and the bee the 'Ancient'. (This was most adroit since in Bacon the spider had been the Medieval Schoolman and the bee the humanistic and scientific modern.) The bee and the spider represent different features of Swift's culture, as they do of our own.

Gulliver, on the face of it, conforms to the paradigm of the bee. In no way does he stay at home working out theories, and is not much impressed by the Laputan theorists who need flappers to remind them of where they are. Active and restless (II. i. 73), drawn by gain and driven by 'my insatiable Desire of seeing foreign Countries' (I. viii. 68), Gulliver is a great traveller like the bee. What he brings home, and what he makes of what he brings home, is another matter. At the end of Part I he brings back miniature cattle; at the end of Part II (among his collection of rarities) was 'a Corn that I had cut off with my own Hand from a Maid of Honour's Toe' (II. viii. 142): he also brings back a distressingly false sense of physical scale. He thinks a little, as we have seen, about the difference of his situation between Lilliput and Brobdingnag. Only at the end of Part IV does Gulliver return home like a man who has, in a moral sense, had a vision of higher things. No other voyage has had this kind of impact on him. The reader may draw some inferences from this. For example, Lilliput, where he performed a great feat, showed his moral superiority and barely escaped wtih his life, does not linger in his mind. Neither does Brobdingnag where he was laughed at and taught such dreadful lessons about his native country. Neither does the wondrous flying island of Laputa. What Gulliver remembers so painfully, in Part IV, is certainly not any lesson which flatters him,

England or Europe. This, perhaps, counts in his favour. Further, the Houyhnhnm ideal is a lived ideal: more innocent than the views of the King of Brobdingnag, it is plain, simple, energetic, kind, a wisdom of practice rather than a wisdom of discourse, though with a capacity for song on the one hand, and a capacity for *realpolitik* (the cause of Gulliver's expulsion) on the other. This stays in his mind as a value, but it is certainly his vision of alternative ways of life, Houyhnhnm and Yahoo, which makes the wisdom he brings home so bitter to him and his family. Of the various choices he has made on his 'unfortunate Voyages' (II. viii. 145) his choice, or perhaps it is his discovery, that he hates the Yahoos and admires the Houyhnhnms is the most painful, because it makes him a stranger to himself. This in itself is not a reason for ridiculing Gulliver; not even, it may be, for condemning him. Other writers have had similar perceptions, though they have expressed them in different ways. One who remembered Swift would write:

> Consume my heart away. Sick with desire
> And fastened to a dying animal
> It knows not what it is ...
>
> (W. B. Yeats, 'Sailing to Byzantium')

What is comic, perhaps, is the characteristic practicality with which Gulliver sets about adjusting to life at home, buying two stallions, talking to his groom, finally allowing his wife to sit at the end of the same table as himself, though here, indeed, the reader is brought back to what Gulliver makes of the wisdom he thinks he has been shown. The bee digests his findings by study, judgement and distinction; Gulliver's problem is that he doesn't sufficiently connect different parts of his own experience, doesn't, for example, connect his knowledge that Yahoos differ and change with his religion which teaches love and redemption. He is a hopeless formalist, admiring horses simply because of the qualities he has previously found horses to embody.

Swift's text, however, will not allow the reader an easy, hand-washing, rejection of the final Gulliver. The last chapter of Part IV is an extraordinary *tour de force*. If he has not sufficiently digested his four voyages, he does recall them all here in connection, characteristically, with invasion and war. This passage (IV. xii. 301–2), the last in the *Travels* in which Gulliver's continuity of character is affirmed, is, significantly, a trenchant criticism of colonization and empire. His account of the origin of the European sea-borne empires could hardly be improved on as a piece of devastating, reductive, humanist satire: the King of Brobdingnag himself could not have put it better, and Montaigne would have recognized a kindred spirit. The passage should stand as a challenge in the annals of empire for ever. Further, the blatant satirical irony of the disclaimer which follows ('But this Description, I confess, doth by no means affect the *British* Nation ...' (IV. xii. 303)) is a mark of moral cunning in Gulliver, and practical sanity. This Gulliver is different from the Gulliver of Part II or even early Part IV. A different note is struck by the two Latin quotations which precede this passage, each from a famous Augustan text, the *Aeneid*, and Horace's satiric dialogue with Trebatius (*Sat.* II. i). When Gulliver quotes:

> Nec si miserum Fortuna Sinonem
> Finxit, vanum etiam, mendacemque improba finget.
>
> *(Aeneid*, II. 79–80)

the proverbial character of the lines ('because I have been unfortunate it does not mean I tell lies') might almost pass without further enquiry, were it not that the name of the speaker, Sinon, reminds those who know the story of the *Aeneid* that it was his lying speech, which these lines introduce, that persuaded the Trojans to admit the wooden horse into their city, thus causing the fall of Troy. It is inconceivable that this notable allusion was not carefully planted by Swift (IV. xii. 300; see Winton, cited in Turner, p. 378), it makes us carry on thinking about horses, but its significance is not without complexity. For example, however, proud or unkind we might judge the final Gulliver to be, he cannot be considered a deliberate political lier like Sinon. Further, the Trojan horse cannot be thought to express the nature of the Houyhnhnms.

Gulliver may have reason to think the Houyhnhnms potentially terrible in war, but warfare by guile would not be their way. This brings us to the point of the allusion. In the *Aeneid* story the guile is that of Ulysses and the other warriors concealed in the wooden horse. It is not a real horse, only an image. Well might King Priam ask:

> 'quo molem hanc immanis equi statuere? quis auctor?
> quidve petunt? quae religio? aut quae machina belli?'
>
> (II. 150–1)

('Why have they set up this massive horse? Who has done it? For what purpose? What religion? Or what engine of war?') The episode emphasizes that it is only the *form* of a horse; and the reader sees that Gulliver fatally confuses truth and reason with the form of the creatures in whom he has found these values. The very strength of his moral feeling has led him to think in terms of images rather than qualities. The Horace quotation, following not long after, displays, less prominently, a similar complexity. There is first the joke that Gulliver should pitch on that point in the famous dialogue which employs the image of a horse: 'Recalcitrat undique tutus' (IV. xii. 302; Turner, p. 378); if you go too far praising Augustus he will kick back at you like a horse (*Sat.* II. i. 20). In an unmistakably Gulliverian paragraph the Houyhnhnms are aligned with Augustus, of whom Gulliver had such a bad impression on the Island of the Ghosts. Does this hint that Gulliver is wrong to admire the Houyhnhnms? It is hard to see that it does. The Augustus who is guilty of ingratitude is to be censured; the Augustus who reacts against excessive praise is to be approved. The allusion tells us more about Gulliver's mind than about the Houyhnhnms. Once again he has not put the different parts of his thought together; his invocation of Augustus here is meant to associate the Houyhnhnms and himself with an image of authority and power with which the republican horses would have been unlikely to be comfortable.

In the order of our reading Swift's last chapter, Gulliver's two Augustan allusions are made before the denunciation of colonizing. Gulliver's frame of mind is thus subtly exposed before the reader is forced to go about and concur in his withering account of modern empire. Then, in the two final paragraphs, his account of the difficulties of his 'Reconcilement to the *Yahoo*-kind in general' (IV.xii.304) is so full of the vanity and pride he is denouncing that we are forced to re-assess our judgement of him for a yet further, and final time; to recognize that, though he has had his vision, which he will never forget, he is no better, is indeed probably worse, than those he condemns. The eucharistic word 'presume' ('that they will not presume to appear in my Sight') reappears in his final sentence.

Gulliver at Redriff should have been some sort of Don Pedro or Mr Rock. Within the simplest pattern of character consistency, Gulliver is forever swinging around, tossed on the seas of circumstance, driven often by his own vanity and egoism, unable to achieve an integrity of experience, though marked by his experience for ever. It is our constant endeavour to reach a lasting conclusion about Gulliver, only to come to a further temporary conclusion about ourselves, which constitutes Swift's irony here. This is far from that rhetorical irony by which Swift is supposed to be distinguished saying the opposite of what he really means with cutting effect, though he does of course employ this device. It is rather the full, radical and dynamic irony which has in recent years been attributed to Romanticism. It keeps the reader constantly active, charting and re-charting a moral line, feeling all the emotion of judge-ments which had had to be abandoned, or have had to be embraced, judgements which, in the end, bear not only on what we think but on what we are.

Chapter 9

The fictional aftermath

A year after the publication of *Gulliver's Travels* the Abbé Désfontaines designated the book 'new and original in its kind' while, simultaneously, a host of literary analogies occurred to him: Plato's *Republic*, Lucian's *True History*, More's *Utopia*, Bacon's *New Atlantis*, Cyrano's *Voyage to the Moon* ... Rabelais' *Pantagruel* (Kathleen Williams, *Heritage*, pp. 80–1). The balance within this reader's mind reminds us that while the thrust of *Gulliver's Travels* itself seems to have created a fresh wake of critical reception, Swift's text is only a current in the broader reception of Plato and Lucian, More and Rabelais. Swift's own critical heritage has been charted by Kathleen Williams to 1819, and by D. M. Berwick to 1882 (see Guide to further reading). Were these surveys to be carried forward into the twentieth century, it is certainly George Orwell, author of 'Politics vs. Literature: An Examination of *Gulliver's Travels*' (1946) and *Animal Farm* (1945), who would dominate any account of the book's recent reception. Something more will be said about Swift and Orwell in this chapter. The tradition of Plato and More has received much attention, that of Rabelais less, while the English heritage of the Renaissance union of critical comedy with the marvellous still awaits adequate assessment. When this is achieved, Coleridge's brilliant *bon mot* on Swift: '*anima Rabelaisii habitans in sicco* – the soul of Rabelais dwelling in a dry place' (*Heritage*, p. 333) will be seen to have put the Enlightenment in its dry place. For it was Voltaire who said that Swift was 'Rabelais in his right senses, and living in good company' (*Heritage*, p. 74).

The most interesting legacy of *Gulliver's Travels* lies less in its critical reception than in fiction itself. Its capacity to produce a creative response was at once seen in Pope's five notable Gulliverian poems (1727), in the Abbé Désfontaines'

Le Nouveau Gulliver (1730) and (an interesting political turn) in the decision to present lightly fictionalized accounts of Parliamentary Debates in the *Gentleman's Magazine* (1738–43), mainly by Samuel Johnson, as *Debates in the Senate of Lilliput*. Swift's book is a special form of fiction, poised between satire, novel, and voyage narrative. Fiction is here closely entangled with generalization, hypothesis and paradox, concerning the nature of the world and the nature of man. It is never far from philosophical play. This kind of writing is quite unlike the rich circumstantial and psychological fiction of the nineteenth century: its genius is to be short and provocative, its purpose to put generalization to the test. Some of the longer fiction of the English eighteenth century touches on this mode, for example the Thwackum and Square sequence of Fielding's *Tom Jones*, where the claims of religion, reason and a good heart are measured against each other, or the more consciously Lockeian episodes of Sterne's *Tristram Shandy*. The individual Parts of *Gulliver's Travels*, and sometimes the relation between its parts, exemplify this kind of fiction. It may be termed the *conte philosophique*.

The year 1759 saw the publication of two such works, Voltaire's *Candide* and Samuel Johnson's *Rasselas*. Each author was familiar with Swift's writings. Voltaire had long been interested in Swift, judging *A Tale of a Tub* to be a satire on religion rather than on abuses in religion, and calling the Swift of the *Travels* 'the English Rabelais' or 'Rabelais perfected'. He saw Swift as a refinement on Rabelais while yet finding tedious Swift's 'continued series' of marvels and wild inventions. He in his turn sought to refine upon Swift. Thus *Candide* rejects the fourfold structure of the *Travels*; the marvellous is replaced by extraordinary coincidence, and the whole effect is lighter, briefer and perhaps wittier than the *Travels*. But, like the *Travels*, it puts a hypothesis to the test: as Swift explores the proposition that man is a rational animal, Voltaire explores the proposition that we live in the best of possible worlds. Neither proposition can withstand experience of the worlds revealed in the fictions of the two authors. It is sometimes said that Voltaire invented the *conte philosophique*. The truth is, he derived it from Swift. The style of the two works has also much in common. Each author seems a lover of prose, sociable, informative, unassuming. Swift's is more pausing, punctuated and thoughtful; Voltaire's, in keeping with his more rapid management of his material and lighter idiom, is the more swift, unerringly precise and entertaining. Johnson's style, by contrast, is utterly different. To turn from *Gulliver's Travels* to *Rasselas* is like turning from the prose of a journal to the verse of *Paradise Lost*. The prose of *Rasselas* is not the shorter style that draws on Tacitus, Seneca and Bacon, but is an inflection of the longer, Ciceronian, periodic style, now made responsive to the sometimes prophetic utterance and parallelistic poetic pattern of the Old Testament. Rasselas, Prince of Abyssinia, meditates as follows on his life in the Happy Valley:

What, said he, makes the difference between man and all the rest of the animal creation? Every beast that strays beside me has the same corporal necessities with myself; he is hungry and crops the grass, he is thirsty and drinks the stream, his thirst and hunger are appeased, he is satisfied and sleeps; he rises again and is hungry, he is again fed and is at rest. I am hungry and thirsty like him, but when thirst and hunger cease I am not at rest; I am, like him, pained with want, but am not, like him, satisfied with fulness. The intermediate hours are tedious and gloomy; I long again to be hungry that I may again quicken my attention. The birds peck the berries or the corn, and fly away to the groves where they sit in seeming happiness on the branches, and waste their lives in tuning one unvaried series of sounds. I likewise can call the lutanist and the singer, but the sounds that pleased me yesterday weary me today, and will grow yet more wearisome to-morrow. I can discover within me no power of perception which is not glutted with its proper pleasure, yet I do not feel myself delighted. Man has surely some latent sense for which this place affords no gratification, or he has some desires distinct from sense, which must be satisfied before he can be happy.

(Ch. II; *Rasselas and Other Tales*, ed. Gwin J. Kolb, *Works*, xvi, 13)

This is different from anything in *Gulliver* or *Candide*. This is eloquence, deliberate, measured, meditative; it sustains itself at length, and does not rise too high, to topple into the ridiculous. We do not, as always in Swift and Voltaire, catch the inflections of the world in the turns and phrases of the prose, even though it aims steadily at the same mark which Swift keeps ever in his sights: what, if anything distinguishes man from beast. That Rasselas, ignorant of all that is beyond the Happy Valley, should speak so tentatively as he does of 'some latent sense' or 'some desires distinct from sense' makes the case for a difference between man and animal far more convincing than any open invocation of doctrine could do.

The three works may be compared in their treatment of the place of happiness. In the *Travels* the happy place is, if anywhere, the country of Gulliver's last voyage, and it is really only Gulliver who is happy there. The Houyhnhnms are rationally content while the Yahoos, driven by appetite and emotion, veer between rage, triumph and self-pity. In *Rasselas* the happy place is the starting point, half Eden, half prison; in *Candide* it is an episode over half-way through the narrative; and is so for a reason. While Voltaire naturally takes the opportunity to compare the world unfavourably with his Eldorado, his wittier and more telling point is that the perfectly happy place can only *be* an episode to someone shaped in the ways of the world. Candide, after almost unimaginable misfortune, might have lived in Eldorado for the rest of his days but, still in quest of his lady Cunégonde, sees the wealth he may take from Eldorado as the means to recovering his loved one. This seems noble if, perhaps, foolish: quixotic; but Voltaire adds some other telling comments. Candide's servant, Cacambo is pleased at his master's decision for, 'on aime tant à courir, à se faire valoir chez les siens, à faire parade de ce qu'on a vu dans ses voyages, que les deux heureux résolurent de ne plus l'être ...' (ch. 18). These remarks say everything. A modern translator has rendered the first words freely as: 'like Candide, he had a restless spirit' but perhaps this formalizes the moment too much. 'One likes so much to keep moving' makes the paradoxical decision sound more like human instinct, which is followed up by observations on the eagerness of the two to boast of their travels. Vanity persuades the happy to be happy no more. The young Rasselas, with as yet no knowledge of the world, no goals, no fears, cannot be happy to be happy, but must experience for himself the changes and chances of a largely miserable world. Gulliver alone, weary with his travels and no longer confident about his own society, wants to stay in the happy place (as he takes the Country of the Houyhnhnms to be). This desire has a deeper psychological grounding than anything in *Candide*, for Gulliver wants to live his difference from the Yahoos and be appreciated for this by a race of rational beings. Yet both Johnson and Voltaire seem to know human nature. All three works are close to philosophical debate about the nature of happiness, and all three are, on the face of it, outrageously paradoxical. Rasselas and Candide reject happiness for some unknown, or uncertain value in the greater world, while Gulliver is happy only in so far as he is like a horse. Each text carries the genius of the *conte philosophique* to the highest pitch: funny, absurd, provocative, serious.

Much as Swift, Johnson and Voltaire have in common, it will be seen that while the *Travels* is consistently the first-person narrative of Lemuel Gulliver, *Rasselas* and *Candide* permit authorial commentary on the decisions and experiences of their chief figures. Stemming from this, perhaps, Swift's development of an ironic viewpoint in the *Travels*, has no rival in Johnson or Voltaire, though each is an adroit manager of local irony. Were we to search the nineteenth century for examples of the *conte philosophique* of ironic viewpoint some interesting examples could be found without any evident connection with Swift, notably James Hogg's *Confessions of a Justified Sinner* (1824) and Henry James' *What Maisie Knew* (1898). These stories bear strongly on philosophical questions of identity, and of moral recognition, without tanging of philosophical argument in the eighteenth-century manner. This is also true of a nineteenth-century fiction which probably does owe a lot to Swift, Herman Melville's *Benito Cereno* (1855), subsequently collected in *Piazza Tales* (1856). It is not just that Melville was, like Swift, a writer of fictional voyages and a describer of imaginary lands, nor even that his early book, *Typee* (1846) turns on illusion and disillusion within the viewpoint of a traveller concerning a primitive people, suggestive though that is. It is rather that the reception of another early book of Melville, *Mardi: And a Voyage Thither*

(1849), was so repeatedly linked with *Gulliver's Travels* by reviewers that it must seem likely that Melville now meditated on the character of Swift's book, if he had not done so before. *Mardi* would have reminded readers particularly of the *Travels*, Part III, partly in its use of the Rabelaisian convention of a voyage to several islands, partly because of its contemporary political allusion. 'We occasionally think of Laputa', said one reviewer; 'it is an outrageous fiction; a transcendental *Gulliver* or *Robinson Crusoe* run mad', said another; a third warned that *Mardi* required 'a wide-awake application' like *Gulliver's Travels*. A fourth invoked the *Travels* and something of its tradition: 'a wonderful and unreadable compound of Ossian and Rabelais − of More's "Utopia" and Harrington's "Oceana", − of "Gulliver's Travels", and Cooks's "Voyages"' (*The Melville Log*, ed. Jay Leyda, I. 293−304). These reviews are hardly complimentary to poor Melville, and are eloquent of the difficulties a nineteenth-century reader might encounter in a highly eclectic and imaginative writer.

The ironic strategy of *Benito Cereno* centres on the candid and gullible mind of the New England Captain Amasa Delano, 'a person of a singularly undistrustful good nature', 'incapable of satire or irony' (pp. 47, 63), who from his sealing ship at anchor off the south coast of Chile, in 1799, sees a very strange vessel entering the bay. Authorial narrative and the impressions of Delano combine to present this ship, partly out of control, perhaps, or in distress, as an emblem of some ancient, alien and declining way of life. Dark figures within the elaborate structures of the vessel suggest a cloistered monastery, while closer inspection reveals an old but once fine Spanish ship, a superseded Acapulco treasure-ship perhaps, or retired naval frigate, which like a superannuated Italian palace 'under a decline of masters, preserved signs of former state' (p. 48). It proves to be a slave ship, whose captain, Don Benito Cereno, ailing, seems scarcely in command. The whole situation on the Spanish ship is disquieting, and the suspicions of the New Englander focus on these representatives of the decadent and treacherous empire of Spain, whose stately symbols are everywhere to be seen. On board the slaver, Delano feels real fear that he may have walked into a murderous trap. He is also baffled by the behaviour of the Africans, though warmly approving the obvious fidelity of Don Benito's black servant Babo. 'Like most men of a good, blithe heart', the reader is later told, 'Captain Delano took to negroes, not philanthropically, but genially, just as other men to Newfoundland dogs' (p. 84). In any case, he has managed to suppress his fears: 'What I, Amasa Delano — Jack of the Beach, as they called me when a lad ... that used to go berrying with cousin Nat and the rest; I to be murdered here at the ends of the earth, on board a haunted pirate-ship by a horrible Spaniard? Too nonsensical to think of!' (p. 77).

After a protracted period of suspense during which Delano fails to come to any interpretation of the signs, the sudden, violent *denouement* reveals that the strange tension on the ship is that of a concealed mutiny of the slaves led by the servant Babo. The murderous intent lay not with the slave-owning Spaniards but the slaves themselves. And finally, filtering out from the documents and depositions about the incident which constitute the end of the *conte*, there briefly emerges the desperate and hopeless purpose of the mutiny: to compel the Spaniards to take their slaves back to Africa, whence they or their forefathers had originally come (pp. 107–8).

Melville's highly coloured style and often Gothic effect, so different from the plain prose of the *Travels*, may make comparison between the two works seem far-fetched. Yet satire and irony are at issue within Melville's tale, since to say that Delano is incapable of satire and irony is to implant in our mind the notion that he might himself become their object — as indeed he does. Within the fissures between deception and self-deception there are two revelations. The first is immediate and physical: the violent intent of the slaves. The second is slow, retrospective, but potent: the realization that the violence of the slaves was not just savagery but a bid for freedom. These may, in the deployment of ironic viewpoint, be paralleled with Gulliver's horrified discovery that he is himself, physically, more or less a Yahoo and recognized as such by the Houyhnhnms; and with our slow later recognition that Yahoos are not uniformly and necessarily bestial. Both Melville and Swift confront the concept of a radical division within human being, rational and irrational, savage and civilized, and it is the blurring of such distinction which is at once so disturbing yet so vitally necessary to recognize. (It may be noted that Melville's earlier Swiftian work, *Mardi*, ch. 157, confirms his critical attitude to the institution of slavery within the United States.)

There are, within the self-conscious, eclectic and experimental twentieth-century novel, fictions to be found which mime eighteenth-century forms and sometimes, also, eighteenth-century settings and content. John Barth's *The Sot-Weed Factor* and William Golding's *Rites of Passage* are examples of the latter group; the former include Thomas Mann's *The Confessions of Felix Krull, Confidence Man* and Nathanael West's *A Cool Million, or, The Dismantling of Lemuel Pitkin* (1934). West is the kind of novelist one would expect to produce such a work, for his four novels, *The Dream Life of Balso Snell, Miss Lonelyhearts*, *A Cool Million* and *The Day of the Locust* are a brilliantly inventive and varied series of fictions. *A Cool Million*, though not his very best, is in style a notable eighteenth-century/twentieth-century *conte philosophique*. The subtitle reminds of Gulliver, while the Candide-like series of disasters which befall the protagonist makes it certain that West is using an eighteenth-century fictional model for modern ends.

The great Spanish inventors of the European novel focused often on the *picaro*, an outcast, rogue or confidence man. This is the strong sense of the term picaresque. The weak sense, denoting simply a loose episodic narrative, applies almost equally to *Candide* and *A Cool Million*. They have something further in common: that eighteenth-century revolution which turned the trickster into Tom Jones or Candide, and turned the world itself into the *picaro* and predator. To enforce this vision West may be thought to transmute the hypothesis that we live in the best of possible worlds into a more specific, historical and cultural form: that America is the best of possible lands, the land of opportunity that never fails the industrious and honest. This America achieves through capitalism, not sinister international capitalism, but thrifty, creative American

capitalism, as exemplified by Henry Ford (p. 150). Lem Pitkin
starts out in life poor but healthy, industrious but innocent.
Advised by Nathan 'Shagpoke' Whipple, President of the Rat
River National Bank, Ottsville, Vermont, to raise a loan on his
mother's cow, Lem sets out for New York where he is robbed,
arrested, punished, and reformed. His subsequent wanderings,
punctuated by *Candide*-like co-incidences, steadily reduce him.
West has a measure of Swift's literalistic, physical, imagination.
America doesn't just ruin young Lem; it really does dismantle
him. He loses his teeth, an eye, his scalp and one leg before,
naively entangled in the Leather Shirts, a fascist movement
founded by Whipple, he is shot by a communist assassin.
It was the government of Lilliput which planned to dismantle
Lemuel Gulliver; Lemuel Pitkin is dismantled by society. His
success is posthumous. The dismantled innocent becomes a
Leather-Shirt martyr, and the *Lemuel Pitkin Song* resounds
down Fifth Avenue, New York, sung by parading thousands:

> A million hearts for Pitkin, oh!
> To do or die with Pitkin, oh!
> To live and fight with Pitkin, oh!
> Marching for Pitkin.

George Orwell, by his own account, had read *Gulliver's
Travels* five or six times when he published *Animal Farm,
A Fairy Story* in August 1945. It may be objected that *Animal
Farm* is not a *conte philosophique* but a beast fable, and thus
falls outside the literary group being explored here. This
objection is answered by the recognition that Orwell's book is
both *conte philosophique* and beast fable, as is 'A Voyage
to the Country of the Houyhnhnms'. In any case, the two forms
have marked affinities, and in Swift's day the beast fable was
so popular that he had no need to signpost his purpose. Like
Part IV of the *Travels* and *Candide*, *Animal Farm* attacks a
well-known generalization; as in *A Cool Million* the generalization has now a modern and historical form. If West shows
up the justice of capitalist America, Orwell shows up the equality
of communist USSR, the ally of Britain and the USA in the
World War which had just ended.

Before concluding this chapter with a brief consideration of George Orwell, we should recognize that the creative impact of *Gulliver's Travels* in the twentieth century is by no means confined to English literature. In German literature the Austrian Karl Kraus, particularly perhaps his *Chinische Mauer* (1964), has suggested a debt to Swift, and an interesting comparative study of Swift and Kraus has been written by J.G. Keith (see Guide to further reading).

In his essay 'Politics vs. Literature' Orwell puts the *Travels* in the half a dozen or so works of literature he would wish above all to be preserved, while at the same time disagreeing with many of the views it seems to recommend. He brilliantly designates Swift a 'Tory anarchist' (*Essays*, IV.216) without particularly admiring this strange combination of qualities. He credits Swift with detecting, in Part III, something of the most destructive aim of totalitarianism, to make people '*less conscious*', but shares the general neo-romantic dislike of the reasonable Houyhnhnms. Just two important points about Orwell's famous satire can be made here. First, the betrayal of the proletarian revolution set forth in *Animal Farm* is not only the exchange of one lot of masters for another just as bad or worse; it is the treacherous suppression of the knowledge that there had ever been a possibility of change. This is the betrayal of '*consciousness*'. It is a more obvious feature of Orwell's text than Swift's, but it is what poor, 'mad', Gulliver is trying to resist when finally home at Redriff. Secondly, Orwell takes what is in his eyes Swift's unattractive positive standard, the rational horses, noting particularly (what Swift often insists on) their physical strength, and turns them into a positive example of a very different kind, Boxer and Clover, Boxer especially, the formidable selfless labourer of the animals' revolution. When Boxer, having worked himself not yet quite to death, is denied his few years' retirement and sold off to the knacker's yard to be made into bone-meal and glue, Orwell, for all his flatter prose style, achieves an emotional *coup* never attempted by Swift, though Swift would have perfectly recognized the motives behind Boxer's extermination.

Orwell is a good writer with whom to conclude this brief survey of the creative aftermath of *Gulliver's Travels* as a landmark in world literature. The *conte philosophique* developed by Voltaire out of the *Travels* remains a single and simple narrative structure. Swift's achievement in the *Travels* is not to have written a single narrative, long or short, nor just a loose collection of four short narratives aiming at a variety of satiric targets. Swift's masterstroke, nowhere repeated, was to hit just that degree of separateness within relatedness, in the four Parts of the *Travels*, to enable the reader's involvement in the narrator's ironic viewpoint, not notable in Voltaire, Johnson, West or Orwell, to constitute in itself an arduous, ever-changing and dangerous voyage of the moral mind, which denies a resting place even at the end.

Endnote

Gulliver's Travels as a book for children

The present author had his children's version, a Christmas present from a kindly aunt in 1941, when he was five years' old. It is *Gulliver's Travels*, by Jonathan Swift, DD, published by Ward, Lock & Co., Ltd, London and Melbourne, no date. There are forty-eight colour plates, including scenes Swift himself recommended for illustration. The text is expurgated and abbreviated. A more notable version is the expurgated but annotated edition published by Cassell and Co., Ltd (London, Paris, New York and Melbourne, 1905) with over 120 illustrations, chiefly by Linton. These are especially spirited in depicting the Houyhnhnms, prompting the speculation that the replacement of the horse by the internal combustion engine as a source of energy has probably facilitated the reaction against the Houyhnhnms in our time.

Guide to further reading

Primary works

Jonathan Swift, *Prose Writings*, ed. Herbert Davis et al., 14 vols.
  (Oxford, 1939–68)
  *Travels Into Several Remote Nations of the World. In Four Parts.
  By Lemuel Gulliver...* (1726), ed. Paul Turner (Oxford, 1971)
  Gulliver's Travels, 1726 text, ed. Angus Ross (London, 1972)
  Gulliver's Travels, reconstructed text with Swift's MS corrections,
  ed. Colin McKelvie (Belfast, 1976)
  Poems, ed. Pat Rogers (Harmondsworth, 1983)
  Correspondence, ed. Sir Harold Williams (Oxford, 1963–5)
Lucian, *The True History*, ed. and tr. A.M. Harmon, Loeb Edn of
  the *Works* (London, 1913)
Petronius Arbiter, *The Satyricon*, tr. William Burnaby and another
  (London, 1694), tr. and intro. William Arrowsmith, Mentor
  (New York, 1959)
Thomas More, *Utopia*, ed. E. Surtz and J.H. Hexter (New Haven,
  1965) vol. iv of the Yale Edn of the *Works. A fruteful and
  pleasaunt works of the beste state of a publique weale, and of
  the newe yle called Vtopia* ... tr. Ralph Robinson (London,
  1551); *The Utopia of Sir Thomas More*, ed. J.H. Lupton
  (Oxford, 1895); new edn intro. Richard Marius, Everyman
  (London, 1985)
  Utopia; Or the Best State of a Commonwealth ... tr. Gilbert
  Burnet (London, 1684)
François Rabelais, *Œuvres Complètes*, ed. Jacques Boulenger and
  Lucien Scheler, Editions Pléiades, Gallimard (1965)
  Pantagruel, ed. V.L. Saulnier (Paris, 1946)
  Gargantua, ed. R.M. Calder and M.A. Screech (Geneva, 1970)
  Le Tiers Livre, ed. M.A. Screech (Geneva, 1964)
  Le Quart Livre, ed. R. Marischal; Textes Littéraires Françaises,
  Droz (Geneva 1947)
  Works of F. Rabelais, M.D.; or *Gargantua and Pantagruel*, tr. Sir
  Thomas Urquhart and P.A. Motteux, 5 vols. (London, 1694);
  Intro. D.B. Wyndham Lewis, Everyman, 2 vols. (London,
  1929), frequently reprinted
Richard Hakluyt, *The Principal Navigations, Voyages and Discoveries*
  ... (London, 1589); reprinted and enlarged 1598–1600)

Samuel Purchas, *Samuel Purchas His Pilgrimage* ... (London, 1613) *Samuel Purchas, His Pilgrim* ... (London, 1619) *Hakluytus Posthumus, Or Purchas His Pilgrimes* (London, 1625)

Joseph Hall, *Mundus Alter et Idem*, tr. John Healey as *The Discovery of a New World* (London, 1609)

Francis Bacon, *The Advancement of Learning*; *The Novum Organum*; *The New Atlantis*; *Works*, ed. J. Spedding, 7 vols. (London, 1861–74)

Cyrano de Bergerac, *Histoire Comique des Etats at Empires de la Lune* ... (1657)

René Descartes, *Discours de la Méthode*; *Méditations*; *Œuvres*, ed. Charles Adam and P. Tannery, 12 vols. (Paris, 1964–76)

Denis Veiras [Denis Vairasse d'Allais], *Histoire des Sévarambes* (1677–9)

Gabriel de Foigny, *La Terre Australe Connue* (1676)

John Bunyan, *The Pilgrim's Progress* ... (London, 1678); ed. Roger Sharrock (Oxford, 1966)

John Flavell, *Navigation Spiritualised* ... (London, ?1682)

William Dampier, *A New Voyage Round the World* ... (London, 1697); Swift owned the 3rd edn, 1698, and signed the title page; ed. Sir Albert Gray (London, 1927)

  A Voyage to New Holland ... (1699); ed. J. A. Williamson (London, 1939)

Daniel Defoe, *The Life and Strange Surprising Adventures of Robinson Crusoe, of York, Mariner*, ed. J. D. Crawley (Oxford, 1972)

Samuel Johnson, *Rasselas, Prince of Abissinia*; *Yale Edition of the Works of Samuel Johnson*, vol. xvi (New Haven and London, 1990); ed. J. P. Hardy, World's Classics (Oxford, 1988)

François-Marie, Arouet, later Voltaire, *Candide, Ou L'Optimisme*, ed. J. H. Brumfitt (Oxford, 1968); tr. John Butt (Harmondsworth, 1947)

Herman Melville, *Benito Cereno* (1855) in *Piazza Tales* (1856); ed. Harrison Hayford, A. A. MacDougall, G. F. Tanselle (Evanston and Chicago, 1987), *Northwestern-Newberry Edition of The Writings of Hermann Melville*, vol. ix (1987); ed. and intro. Harold Beaver, *Billy Budd the Sailor and other Stories*, Penguin (Harmondsworth, 1967)

Jay Leyda, ed. *The Melville Log: A Documentary Life of Herman Melville, 1819–1891* (New York, 1951; expanded 1969)

Nathanael West, *A Cool Million, Or The Dismantling of Lemuel Pitkin* (1934); *Complete Works*, intro. Alan Ross (London, 1957)

George Orwell, *Animal Farm, A Fairy Story* (1945), ed. Malcolm Bradbury and Peter Davison (Harmondsworth, 1989)

Henry Green, *Concluding* (London, 1948)

Secondary works
(in chronological order of publication)

(i) *Bibliographical works*

L. A. Landa and J. E. Tobin, eds. *Jonathan Swift: A List of Critical Studies from 1895 to 1945* (New York, 1945)

J. J. Stathis, *A Bibliography of Swift Studies, 1945–65* (Nashville, Tenn., 1967)

R. H. Rodino, *Swift Studies, 1965–1980, An Annotated Bibliography* (New York, 1984)

(ii) *Biographical and critical works on Swift*

John Boyle, Fifth Earl of Orrery, *Remarks on the Life and Writing of Dr Jonathan Swift* (London, 1752)

Patrick Delaney, *Observations on Lord Orrery's Remarks* (London, 1754)

C. H. Firth, 'The Political Significance of Gulliver's Travels', *Proceedings of the British Academy*, 9 (London, 1919)

W. A. Eddy, *Gulliver's Travels: A Critical Study* (Princeton, 1923)

Carl Van Doren, *Swift* (London, 1931)

Ricardo Quintana, *The Mind and Art of Jonathan Swift* (London, 1936)

D. M. Berwick, *The Reputation of Jonathan Swift, 1781–1882* (Philadelphia, 1941)

A. E. Case, *Four Essays on Gulliver's Travels* (Princeton, 1945)

George Orwell, 'Politics vs. Literature: An Examination of *Gulliver's Travels*' (1946), republished in *Shooting an Elephant* (1950); *Essays, Journalism and Letters*, ed. S. Orwell and I. Angus, 4 vols. (London, 1968)

Herbert Davis, *The Satire of Jonathan Swift* (New York, 1947)

F. R. Leavis, 'The Irony of Swift', in *The Common Pursuit* (London, 1952)

W. B. Ewald, *The Masks of Swift* (Oxford, 1952)

J. M. Bullitt, *Jonathan Swift and the Anatomy of Satire* (Cambridge; Mass., 1953)

Martin Price, *Swift's Rhetorical Art* (New Haven, 1953)

Roland M. Frye, 'Swift's Yahoo and the Christian Symbols for Sin', *Journal of the History of Ideas*, 15, 1954

L. L. Landa, *Swift and the Church of Ireland* (Oxford, 1954)

E. D. Leyburn, *Satiric Allegory: The Mirror of Man* (New Haven, 1956)

Michael Foot, *The Pen and the Sword* (London, 1957)

Irvin Ehrenpreis, *The Personality of Jonathan Swift* (London, 1958)

Norman O. Brown, 'The Excremental Vision', in *Life Against Death* (Middletown, Conn. 1959)

Samuel Holt Monk, 'The Pride of Lemuel Gulliver', in *Eighteenth-Century English Literature*, ed. J.L. Clifford (London, 1959)

Kathleen Williams, *Swift and the Age of Compromise* (London, 1959)

R.C. Elliott, *The Power of Satire* (Princeton, 1960)

J.A. Traugott, 'A Voyage to Nowhere with Thomas More and Swift: *Utopia* and the Voyage to the Houyhnhnms', *Sewanee Review*, 49, 1961

M.P. Foster, ed. *A Casebook on Gulliver Among the Houyhnhnms* (New York, 1961)

Philip Harth, *Swift and Anglican Rationalism* (Chicago, 1961)

R.S. Crane, 'The Houyhnhnms, the Yahoos, and the History of Ideas', in *Reason and Imagination: Essays in the History of Ideas, 1600–1800*, ed. Joseph R. Mazzeo (London, 1962)

O.W. Ferguson, *Swift and Ireland* (Urbana, 1962)

Irvin Ehrenpreis, *Swift, the Man, his Works and the Age*, 3 vols. (London, 1962–83)

E.W. Rosenheim, *Swift and the Satirist's Art* (Chicago, 1963)

E.L. Tuveson, ed. *Swift: A Collection of Critical Essays*; *Twentieth-Century Views* (Englewood Cliffs, 1964)

Milton Voight, *Swift and the Twentieth Century* (Detroit, 1964)

Roger McHugh and Philip Edwards, eds. *Jonathan Swift, 1667–1967: A Dublin Tercentenary Tribute* (Dublin, 1967)

Denis Donoghue, *Jonathan Swift: A Critical Introduction* (London, 1969)

M.M. Kelsall, 'Iterum Houyhnhnm: Swift's Sextumvirate and the Horses' (1969), in Richard Gravil, ed. *Swift, Gulliver's Travels, A Casebook* (London, 1974)

Martin Kallich, *The Other End of the Egg: Religious Satire in Gulliver's Travels* (Bridgeport, Conn. 1970)

Kathleen Williams, ed. *Swift: The Critical Heritage* (London, 1971)

C.J. Rawson, *Focus: Swift* (London, 1971)

G. Douglas Atkins, 'Pope and Deism: A New Analysis', *Huntington Library Quarterly*, 35 (1972), 257–78

C.J. Rawson, *Gulliver and the Gentle Reader: Studies in Swift and Our Time* (London, 1973; paperback, New Jersey and London, 1991)

Richard Gravil, ed. *Swift: Gulliver's Travels: A Casebook* (London, 1974)

J.G. Keith, 'A Comparison of Jonathan Swift's and Karl Kraus's Pro-Satire; a Contribution to the Theory of Satire' (unpublished Cambridge PhD dissertation, 1974)

Jenny Mezciems, 'The Unity of Swift's "Voyage to Laputa": Structure as Meaning in Utopian Fiction', *Modern Language Review*, 72 (Jan. 1977), 1–21

Clive Probyn, ed. *The Art of Jonathan Swift* (London, 1978)

Peter Steele, *Jonathan Swift: Preacher and Jester* (Oxford, 1978)

F.P. Lock, *The Politics of Gulliver's Travels* (London, 1980)

Carole Fabricant, *Swift's Landscape* (Baltimore, 1982)

Patrick Reilly, *Jonathan Swift: The Brave Desponder* (Manchester, 1982)

A.C. Elias, *Swift at Moor Park* (Philadelphia, 1982)

C.J. Rawson, *The Character of Swift's Satire: A Revised Focus* (London, 1983)

E. Zimmerman, *Swift's Narrative Satires: Author and Authority* (Ithaca, N.Y., 1983)

J.A. Downie, *Jonathan Swift: Political Writer* (London, 1984)

C.J. Rawson, *Order from Confusion Sprung* (London, 1985; paperback, New Jersey and London, 1991)

David Nokes, *Jonathan Swift: A Hypocrite Reversed* (Oxford, 1985)

Brean Hammond, *Gulliver's Travels* (Milton Keynes, 1988)

J.A. Rembert, *Swift and the Dialectical Tradition* (New York, 1988)

C.H. Flynn, *The Body in Swift and Defoe* (Cambridge, 1990)

(iii) *Related critical and philosophical works*

Gilbert Ryle, *The Concept of Mind* (London, 1949)

Rosalie L. Colie, *Paradoxica Epidemica: The Renaissance Tradition of Paradox* (Princeton, 1966)

Frank Manuel, ed. *Utopias and Utopian Thought* (Boston, Mass. 1967)

John Dunn, *The Political Thought of John Locke* (Cambridge, 1969)

Dominic Baker-Smith, *Thomas More and Plato's Voyage* (Cardiff, 1978)

M.A. Screech, *Rabelais* (London, 1979)

Richard A. McCabe, *Joseph Hall: A Study of Satire and Meditation* (Oxford, 1982)

Rod Mengham, *The Idiom of the Time: The Writings of Henry Green* (Cambridge, 1982)

H. Erskine-Hill, *The Augustan Idea in English Literature* (London, 1983)

C.J. Rawson (assisted by Jenny Mezciems), *English Satire and the Satiric Tradition* (Oxford, 1984)

Pat Rogers, *Literature and Popular Culture in Eighteenth-Century England* (London, 1985)

(iv) *Related historical works*

J.P. Kenyon, *The Stuarts* (London, 1958)

Revolution Principles: The Politics of Party, 1689–1720 (Cambridge, 1977)

Stuart England (Harmondsworth, 1978)

Geoffrey Holmes, *British Politics in the Age of Anne* (London, 1967)

G. V. Bennett, *The Tory Crisis in Church and State, 1688–1730* (Oxford, 1977)

Jonathan Clark, *English Society, 1688–1832* (Cambridge, 1985)

James Sambrook, *The Eighteenth Century: The Intellectual and Cultural Context of English Literature, 1700–1789* (London, 1986)

Conrad Russell, *The Causes of the English Civil War* (Oxford, 1990)

Isabel Rivers, *Reason, Grace and Sentiment: A Study of the Language of Religion and Ethics in England, 1660–1780* (Cambridge, 1991)

Manuel Schonhorn, *Defoe's Politics: Parliament, Power, Kingship, and Robinson Crusoe* (Cambridge, 1991)